QUICK & EASY
MICROWAVING™
SECRETS

Developed By The Kitchens Of The  MICROWAVE COOKING INSTITUTE®

D0521377

Library of Congress Cataloging-in-Publication Data

Quick & Easy Microwaving Secrets.

Includes index. 1. Microwave Cookery. I. Title: Quick & Easy
Microwaving Secrets.
TX832.Q53   1986   641.5'882   86-16612
ISBN 0-86573-525-5
ISBN 0-86573-527-1 (pbk.)

Published by Prentice Hall Press
A Division of Simon & Schuster, Inc., New York
ISBN 0-13-749672-9

Contents

No longer a novelty appliance, the microwave oven is fast becoming standard equipment in today's kitchen. It's a worthwhile investment when you discover that the advantages of having a microwave go far beyond reheating pizza and defrosting frozen dinners. You can use it alone or with other appliances (including your present oven/range) — for quick and easy meals, snacks and treats.

This picture-loaded book will help make you knowledgeable about the basics of microwave cooking and skilled in the secrets of preparing a wide variety of foods with perfect results.

Recipes show you how to prepare popular foods the quick and easy way, with tips, short-cuts and appealing serving ideas.

Begin by reading the literature that came with your oven. Microwave ovens vary dramatically in size and power levels, and this makes a big difference in cooking times. If you know what your manufacturer recommends, you'll be able to choose the correct settings from our flexible recipe instructions.

Now, get ready to make the most of your microwave!

The 6 Basic Facts of Microwaving

1 **Fat, water and sugar.** Certain ingredients heat up quickly. All food molecules absorb microwave energy. This energy makes them move at incredible speed, which creates friction, which in turn cooks the food. Fat, water and sugar molecules are especially receptive to microwaves, so foods which contain more of these get hot in a hurry — fat-streaked meat, juicy apples and sweet rolls, for instance.

2 Covering. Covers trap moisture, speed cooking and help prevent spatters. If you want to retain the most moisture for fast-cooking, steaming and tenderizing, use a dish with a fitted cover, or use plastic wrap. (With plastic wrap, leave a steam vent at one edge to prevent the plastic from splitting.) Cooking bags let you microwave food totally in its own good moisture . . . great for tenderizing meats. To retain just a little heat and moisture, cover the food with a piece of wax paper. To keep food from spattering in the oven, cover it with a paper towel. To keep baked goods from getting soggy, wrap them in a paper towel, which will absorb the moisture as they heat.

3 Arranging and rearranging. Food at the outside edges of the dish receives more micro-wave energy than food at the center. When you can, you should arrange thick parts toward the edges and corners, and thin or faster-cooking ends toward the center. Place multiple items (potatoes, cupcakes) in a ring pattern. Rearrange foods during cooking — center parts to the edges and vice versa. Rotate foods which can't be rearranged or stirred (lasagna), or turn over large foods (a whole cauliflower). Stir sauces, eggs, vegetables and casseroles at least once during cooking time.

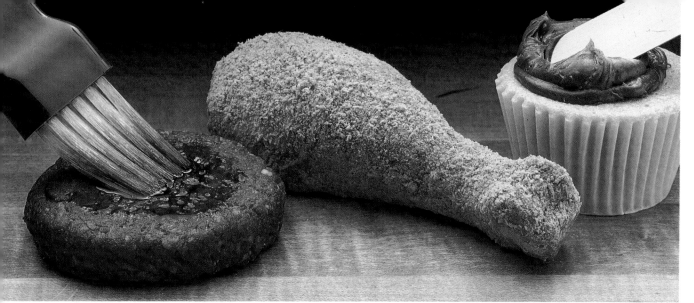

4 Browning. Because microwaving is a moist cooking system, meats don't usually brown, cakes don't crust, and colors of some perfectly cooked foods may seem pale to you. However, there are a number of browning agents you can use to make foods look more appetizing. Soy, barbecue, and gravy-making sauces can be brushed on chicken and hamburgers before cooking. Ham and chicken can be glazed with jellies. Meat can also be rolled in coatings of cereal crumbs, crushed potato chips, dry mixes, grated Parmesan cheese or shake-on products for a darker, crunchy look. You can always sear and brown meats with your conventional oven-range before you add them to the microwave recipe. Cakes and cupcakes can be frosted or topped with coconut, candies, or whipped cream.

6 Utensils. Glass, ceramic, hard plastic and paper are materials through which microwaves can pass. Be sure they are labeled microwave-safe, or test them by putting the dish and a measuring cup of water in your oven and microwaving for 1 minute at High. If the dish becomes hot, it is not safe. Paper towels, all-paper packages, and paper plates are especially convenient for microwave heating. Wooden spoons can even be left in the bowl during microwaving. Special microwave racks, bowls and pans are made of hard plastic. (Other

5 Doneness tests. Test for doneness after microwaving, or after "standing time" when recipes call for the food to "stand" to complete cooking. Test as you always do: with meats, fish, potatoes or vegetables, use a fork to judge the texture; with cakes, notice if they have pulled slightly away from the edge of the dish and if the initial surface moisture has evaporated; with custard, insert a knife to see if it comes out clean. Every recipe in this book includes a test for doneness. After some practice following recipes, you will be able to tell how much time foods need in *your* oven, in order to be cooked to *your* preference. You will frequently remove foods from the oven before they appear completely done. Avoid overcooking. If foods need additional cooking time after standing, they can easily go back for more microwaving.

plastics can be used for heating and defrosting, but they may discolor or distort.) To cook more evenly, many microwave containers are ring-shaped, so that energy penetrates food from the center as well as from the outside edges.

Don't use metal. Metals reflect the energy away from foods and may cause electrical sparking. Don't use metal twist-ties or gold-rimmed plates. (But small pieces of aluminum foil are fine for shielding more vulnerable areas.) Only made-for-microwave thermometers should be used inside your oven.

Defrosting

How to Defrost Frozen Pouches

Flex frozen pouches and packages which cannot be broken up or stirred while cooking, to allow even heat distribution. Pierce pouch with a knife before microwaving, to allow steam to escape.

The delight of being able to microwave foods quickly is only exceeded by the convenience of being able to thaw frozen foods on a moment's notice. In fact, meats thawed in the microwave just before cooking retain more moisture and taste, and suffer less flavor loss, than meats thawed conventionally.

Use your Defrost setting or a 30% (Medium Low) or 50% (Medium) power setting, as indicated in the recipes in this book.

How to Defrost Ground Beef

1 Remove ground beef from package and place in a casserole. Divide total defrosting time as indicated in chart (inside back cover) into 3 equal segments.

2 Remove defrosted portions of meat after each segment of defrosting time. If any frozen meat remains after last segment let stand for 5 to 10 minutes, or until softened but still cold.

How to Defrost Chicken Pieces

1 Unwrap chicken and place on a roasting rack. Defrost for half the time indicated on chart (inside back cover). Separate chicken pieces.

2 Rearrange chicken pieces so that meatiest portions are toward outside. Defrost for remaining time; let stand for 5 to 10 minutes, or until chicken is pliable but still cold. Rinse under cold running water.

How to Defrost Fish Fillets, Steaks & Small Whole Fish

1 Defrost for half the time indicated in chart (inside back cover). Remove fish pieces from package, and separate the pieces. Place fish pieces in a baking dish.

2 Rearrange fish pieces so less-defrosted parts are brought to the top and outside edges of dish. Defrost for remaining time, or until the fish is pliable but still icy inside. Let stand for 5 minutes; rinse under cold running water.

Reheating

Reheating food in a microwave is so successful you can't tell leftovers from freshly cooked servings. Foods reheat quickly with minimum moisture loss and better flavor retention. For feeding family members who eat at different hours, for preparing meals in advance, and for enjoying the contents of restaurant "doggie bags," reheating foods by microwave is a real convenience.

Reheat most foods at a lower power level, so that they warm without unwanted overcooking.

Arrange plates of food so that thick, dense foods are toward the outside and delicate foods toward the center of the plate.

Cover main dishes and casseroles. If they have been refrigerated, microwave at High for a few minutes, then reduce power to finish reheating.

Wrap moist foods, such as vegetables, to retain moisture and assure fresh taste.

Stir main dishes and casseroles, if possible, to distribute heat equally and speed reheating.

Rotate main dishes which cannot be stirred, and microwave them at 50% (Medium).

Spread main dishes out to an even, shallow layer to assure quick, uniform heating.

Test by feeling bottom of plate. Food is ready when it is hot enough to transfer heat to plate.

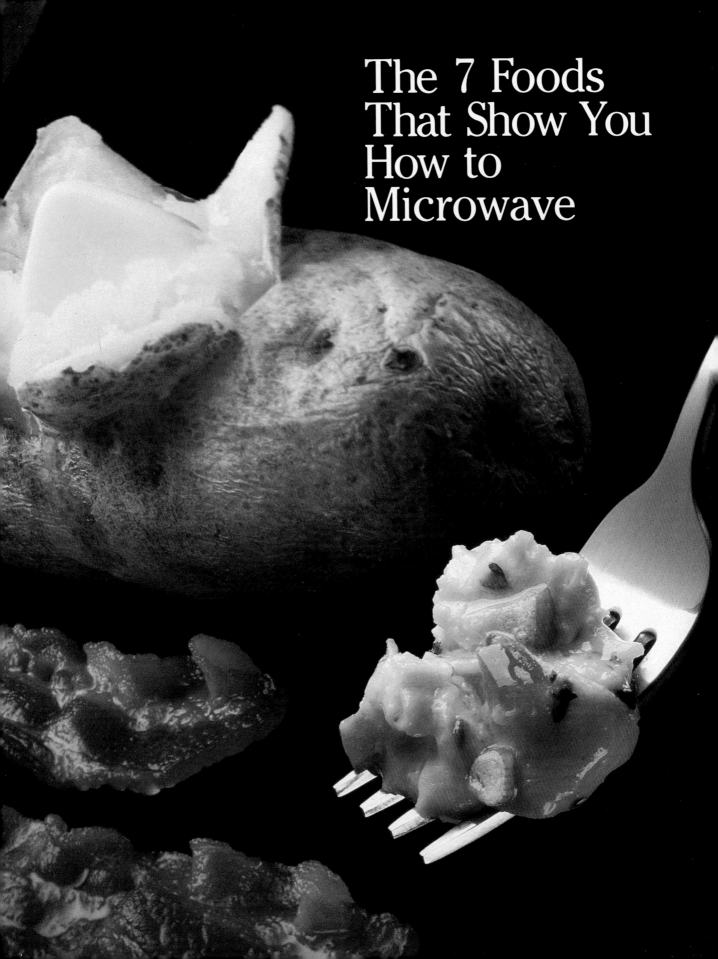

The 7 Foods That Show You How to Microwave

1. Instant Hot Drinks

Microwave at High:	Time:
1 cup water	2-3 minutes
2 cups water	4-5 minutes
3 cups water	6½-7 minutes

◄ Cappuccino

Fill a coffee cup or mug half full with hot tap water. Microwave at High for 1½ to 3 minutes, or until the water boils. Stir in 1 teaspoon of instant espresso coffee. Add enough milk to fill the cup. Microwave at High for 30 seconds to 1 minute, or until the liquid is hot. If desired, top with whipped cream and a dash of ground cinnamon.

1 serving

Total Cooking Time: 2 to 4 minutes

Mocha Coffee

½ cup instant cocoa mix
¼ cup instant coffee crystals
4 cups hot tap water

4 servings

In a 2-quart casserole, combine the cocoa mix, coffee crystals and hot tap water. Stir until blended; cover. Microwave at High for 4 to 8 minutes, or until the liquid is hot, stirring after half the cooking time. If desired, garnish with whipped cream and chocolate curls.

Total Cooking Time: 4 to 8 minutes

Sunny Tea ▲

1 can (6 oz.) frozen pineapple-orange juice concentrate
¼ cup instant lemon-flavored tea powder
2 tablespoons packed brown sugar
½ teaspoon ground cinnamon
¼ teaspoon ground nutmeg
5 cups hot tap water

6 servings

1 Place the frozen pineapple-orange juice concentrate in a 2-quart casserole. Microwave at High for 1 minute to defrost.

2 Stir in the lemon-flavored tea powder, brown sugar, cinnamon and nutmeg until mixture is smooth. Add the hot tap water, stirring to blend. Cover.

3 Microwave at High for 8 to 10 minutes, or until the liquid is hot, stirring after half the cooking time. If desired, garnish tea with lemon slices.

Total Cooking Time: 9 to 11 minutes

2. Perfect Bacon

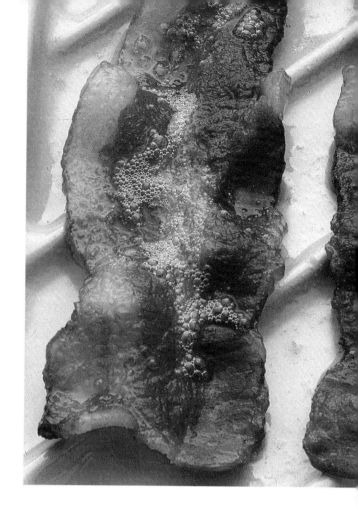

Bacon is always a great microwave success. It cooks up faster, cleaner, leaner and prettier than it does in the frying pan. Because it's fat and it's flat, it cooks evenly and becomes crisp without overcooking. For thick-sliced bacon, add a little extra cooking time.

Of the two methods shown here, the Roasting Rack Method will give you bacon that's a little more curly and moist. The choice is yours.

Microwave at High:	Time:
2 slices	1½-2½ minutes
4 slices	3-6 minutes
6 slices	3-7 minutes

How to Microwave Bacon

1 Layer 3 paper towels directly on the oven floor or on a paper plate. (To microwave bacon in layers, line a baking dish with paper towels.)

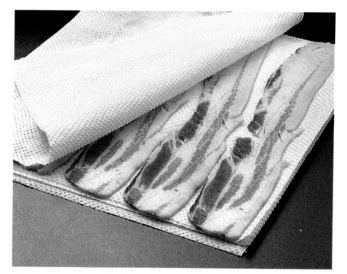

2 Arrange 2 to 6 slices of bacon on the paper towels and cover with another paper towel. (For layers of bacon, cover each layer with paper towel.) Microwave as directed in chart (above).

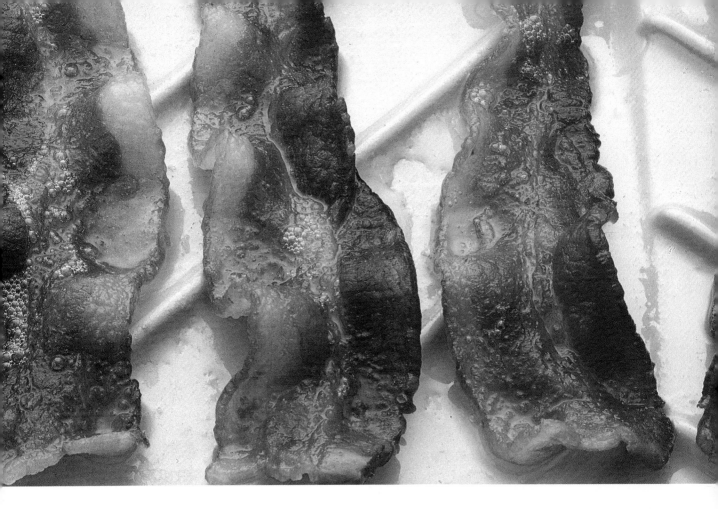

Roasting Rack Method

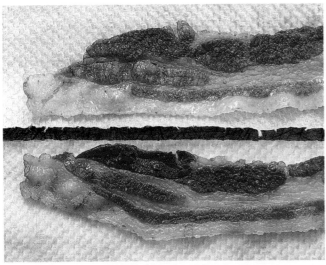

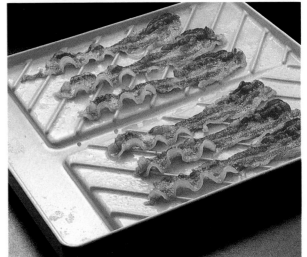

3 Remove the bacon from the oven when it is just crisp and golden brown. Let stand for 1 to 2 minutes. After standing, bacon will be evenly cooked.

Microwave bacon on a microwave roasting rack when you wish to save drippings, or if you prefer less crisp bacon.

◄ Bacon Stix

6 slices bacon
¼ cup grated Parmesan cheese
6 thin bread sticks (any flavor) 8 inches long

6 bacon stix

Follow photo directions below.

Total Cooking Time: 4 to 5½ minutes

Preparation Tip:
Bacon Stix can be assembled in advance
and will stay crisp for several hours after
microwaving.

How to Microwave Bacon Stix

1 Dredge one side of each bacon strip in cheese, then roll it around a bread stick, cheese-side in.

2 Place sticks on a baking sheet, dish, or roasting rack lined with paper towels. Microwave at High for 4 to 5½ minutes, or until bacon begins to brown. Roll again in cheese.

Greens with Bacon ▲

4 slices bacon, cut into ¾-inch pieces
¼ cup chopped onion
½ teaspoon lemon juice
⅛ teaspoon salt
　Dash nutmeg
　Dash pepper
1 lb. fresh greens (collard, mustard or turnip)
　torn into bite-size pieces

4 servings

1 Combine the bacon and onion in a 3-quart casserole. Microwave at High for 4 to 8 minutes, or until the bacon is crisp, stirring once during cooking time.

2 Mix in the lemon juice and seasonings. Add greens; toss to coat. Cover. Microwave at High for 4 to 6 minutes, or until the greens are tender, stirring once during cooking time.

Total Cooking Time: 8 to 14 minutes

Sweet-Sour Spinach ▲

4 slices bacon, cut into ¾-inch pieces
1 tablespoon packed brown sugar
1 tablespoon all-purpose flour
¼ teaspoon dry mustard
¼ teaspoon salt
　Dash pepper
½ cup half-and-half
1 tablespoon cider vinegar
1 lb. fresh spinach, torn into bite-size pieces

4 servings

1 In a 3-quart casserole, microwave the bacon at High for 3 to 5 minutes, or until lightly browned. Drain all but 1 tablespoon of the bacon drippings. Stir in the brown sugar, flour and seasonings. Blend in half-and-half.

2 Microwave at High for 1 to 3 minutes, or until the mixture thickens, stirring once during cooking time. Mix in vinegar and spinach; toss to coat. Microwave at High for 2 to 6 minutes longer, or until spinach is just tender, stirring after half the cooking time.

Total Cooking Time: 6 to 14 minutes

3. One-dish Scrambled Eggs

Microwave-scrambled eggs are fluffier; and you can stir, cook and serve them in the same dish! Cook them as you like them — soft or firm — but remove them while they are still slightly undercooked. You can always put them back for a few seconds more, but overcooking makes eggs rubbery. **Never microwave eggs in the shells; built-up steam will burst them.**

The recipes on the next pages will help you create your own favorite dishes. If you're counting calories, omit the butter, and substitute water for milk.

Microwave at High:	Time:
1 large egg	35 seconds-1 minute
2 large eggs	1¼-1¾ minutes
4 large eggs	2-3¼ minutes

Allow 1-2 minutes standing time.

How to Microwave Scrambled Eggs

1 In a small casserole, microwave 1 tablespoon butter at High for 30 seconds. Add eggs and 1 to 2 tablespoons milk.

2 Scramble the mixture with a fork. Microwave as directed in chart (above), stirring 2 or 3 times during cooking.

3 Remove eggs from oven while they are still soft and moist. Let them stand for 1 to 2 minutes to complete cooking.

4 Eggs will be set after standing. If you prefer firmer eggs, microwave them for a few seconds longer. Stir before serving.

Scrambled Eggs in a Mug ▲

1 tablespoon butter or margarine
1 or 2 large eggs
1 tablespoon milk or water
Dash salt
Dash pepper

1 serving

1 In a 12-oz. microwave-safe mug, microwave the butter at High for 45 seconds to 1 minute, or until melted. Add the egg, milk, salt and pepper. Stir or whip with a fork.

2 Microwave at High as directed in chart (page 21), or until the eggs begin to set, stirring to break the eggs apart once during cooking time. Remove eggs while they are still soft and moist. Let stand for 1 to 2 minutes, or until eggs are set. If desired, sprinkle with shredded cheese and crumbled cooked bacon during standing time.

Total Cooking Time: 1¼ to 2¾ minutes

Santa Fe Scrambled Eggs ▲

4 large eggs
¼ teaspoon dried parsley flakes
¼ teaspoon dried oregano leaves
¼ teaspoon salt
⅛ teaspoon black pepper
¼ cup chopped green pepper
2 green onions, sliced
1 small tomato, chopped
½ cup shredded Monterey Jack cheese

4 servings

1 Beat the eggs and spices together in a medium bowl. Stir in green pepper, onions and tomato. Microwave mixture at High for 3½ to 5 minutes, or until the eggs are soft-set, stirring 2 or 3 times during cooking.

2 Sprinkle eggs with Monterey Jack cheese; cover. Let eggs stand for 1 to 2 minutes, or until the cheese melts.

Total Cooking Time: 3½ to 5 minutes

Open Face Omelet

1 tablespoon butter or margarine
4 large eggs, separated
¼ teaspoon salt
⅛ teaspoon pepper

4 servings

1 In a 9-inch pie plate, microwave the butter at High for 45 seconds to 1 minute, or until melted. In a medium bowl, beat the egg whites until stiff but not dry. Beat yolks lightly in a small bowl. Add salt and pepper, then fold yolk mixture gently into beaten whites. Pour mixture into pie plate.

2 Microwave at 50% (Medium) for 5 to 8 minutes, or until eggs are partially set. Lift edges of pie plate to spread uncooked portion.

3 If desired, sprinkle with shredded cheese. Microwave at 50% (Medium) for 1 minute, or until cheese melts.

Total Cooking Time: 6¾ to 10 minutes

Broccoli Provolone Omelet ▲

1 recipe Open Face Omelet (left)
1 cup chopped cooked broccoli, drained
1 to 2 oz. Provolone (or mozzarella) cheese, sliced into thin strips

4 servings

1 Prepare Open Face Omelet as directed (left). Place cooked broccoli on omelet; top with Provolone cheese strips.

2 Microwave at 50% (Medium) for 1 to 2 minutes, or until the cheese melts.

Total Cooking Time: 7½ to 12 minutes

Hard-cook Eggs:
To hard-cook eggs for chopping and adding to recipes, crack one egg into small bowl. Prick yolk. Cover with plastic wrap. Microwave at 50% (Medium) for 1¾ to 2 minutes, or until yolk is almost set. Let stand, covered, for 1 minute to complete cooking.

4. Baked Potato in 5 Minutes

You no longer have to plan ahead to include baked potatoes with your meal. They are one of the marvels of microwaving.

A potato microwaves in about 5 minutes, and must stand about 5 minutes more to complete cooking. When you pop them open, you'll be pleased with the even, flaky texture throughout.

Microwave at High:	Time:
1 potato	3-6½ minutes
2 potatoes	5-10 minutes
4 potatoes	10-16 minutes

Allow 5 minutes standing time.

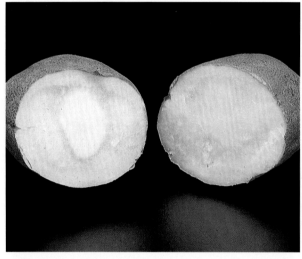

Uncooked center (left) remains after 5 minutes of microwaving. After standing 5 minutes, the center is completely cooked (right).

How to Microwave Baked Potatoes

1 Prick each potato. If desired, wrap each in a paper towel or arrange on roasting rack. Microwave at High as directed in chart (above), or until potatoes are soft to the touch, turning over once during cooking time.

2 Let stand for 5 minutes to complete cooking. Potatoes wrapped in aluminum foil will stay warm for 45 minutes.

Stuffed Potato Shells

 2 potatoes (8 to 10 oz. each)
¼ teaspoon salt
⅛ teaspoon pepper
¼ cup sour cream
½ cup shredded Cheddar cheese
 1 tablespoon sliced green onion
 1 slice bacon, cooked and crumbled

4 servings

Follow photo directions, opposite.

Total Cooking Time: 7½ to 17 minutes

Variations:

Parmesan Chicken Shells:
Follow recipe for Stuffed Potato Shells, except:
add ½ cup finely chopped cooked chicken;
substitute ¼ cup grated Parmesan cheese for
the Cheddar cheese.

Mexican Potato Shells:
Follow recipe for Stuffed Potato Shells, except:
substitute Monterey Jack cheese for the Cheddar
cheese; substitute 2 tablespoons canned
chopped green chives for the crumbled bacon;
serve with taco or salsa sauce.

How to Microwave Stuffed Potato Shells

1 Scrub potatoes, then pierce. Arrange on a roasting rack or wrap each in a paper towel. Microwave at High for 5 to 10 minutes, or until soft to the touch, turning over after half the cooking time. Let potatoes stand for 5 minutes to complete cooking.

2 Slice each potato lengthwise in half, then crosswise. Carefully scoop out centers, leaving ¼ inch of potato next to skin. Arrange skins on serving plate.

3 Sprinkle potato shells with salt and pepper. Spread thin layer of sour cream in each shell. Sprinkle shells with Cheddar cheese, green onion and crumbled bacon.

4 Microwave at 50% (Medium) for 2½ to 7 minutes, or until the cheese melts, rotating plate once during cooking time.

5. Hot Dogs: One-minute Easy

Use the special paper towel wrap to get the hot dog hot all the way through, and the bun warm (but not soggy).

Microwave at High:	Time:
1 hot dog	30 seconds-1 minute
2 hot dogs	45 seconds-1½ minutes
4 hot dogs	1¾-2½-minutes

How to Microwave Hot Dogs

1 Place hot dog in a bun. Wrap hot dog in a paper towel. Microwave hot dog at High as directed in chart (above).

2 Rearrange once when heating more than 1 hot dog, moving outside hot dogs to center. When heating hot dogs without buns, the microwave times will be slightly shorter.

Chili Cheese Dogs

4 hot dogs
4 hot dog buns
½ cup prepared chili
2 slices (¾ oz. each) American cheese, cut
    in half

4 servings

1 Place hot dogs in buns and arrange them in a paper-towel-lined dish.

2 Top each hot dog with 2 tablespoons chili and one piece of cheese.

3 Microwave at High for 2 to 5 minutes, or until the cheese melts, rotating dish twice during cooking time.

Total Cooking Time: 2 to 5 minutes

Variations:

Kraut Dogs:
Follow recipe for Chili Cheese Dogs, except: mix ½ cup sauerkraut and 2 tablespoons sweet pickle relish; substitute for prepared chili and American cheese slices; microwave as directed.

Bacon & Cheese Dogs:
Follow recipe for Chili Cheese Dogs, except: omit the prepared chili and American cheese slices; top each cooked hot dog with 1 tablespoon each of pasteurized process cheese spread and cooked crumbled bacon.

Taco Dogs:
Follow recipe for Chili Cheese Dogs, except: omit the prepared chili and American cheese slices; top each hot dog with 1 tablespoon of taco sauce and 1 tablespoon shredded Cheddar cheese. Sprinkle ½ cup of crushed taco chips over the hot dogs, and microwave as directed. If desired, top hot dogs with shredded lettuce and chopped tomato before serving.

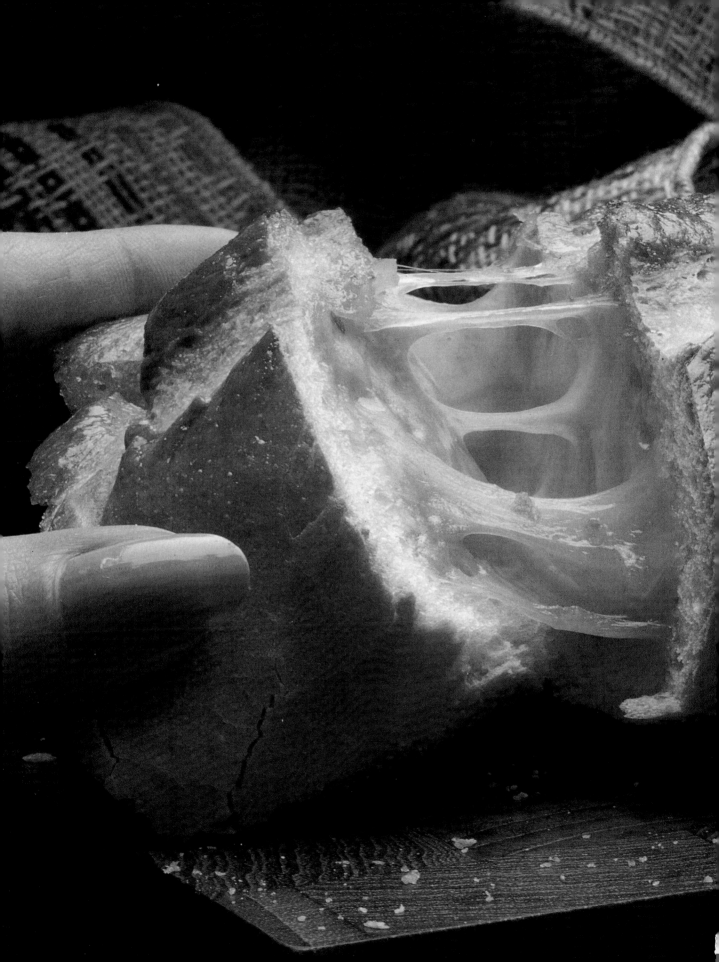

6. Shortcuts to Hot Breads

You can enhance bakery breads with cheeses, herbs and other flavors, and meld them in the microwave. A few seconds' warming can give a new lift to bread, bagels, biscuits, muffins, rolls or buns. They won't get soggy if you wrap them in paper towels, and they'll stay tender if you don't overheat them.

◄ Cheese French Bread

1 French roll (about 4 oz.) 7 inches long
1 slice (¾ oz.) American, Colby or mozzarella
    cheese, cut diagonally into 4 triangles
                                    1 to 2 servings

1 Cut the French roll diagonally at 1½-inch intervals, just to within ½ inch of the bottom crust. Insert one triangle of cheese into each slit. Wrap the roll in a paper towel.

2 Microwave at 50% (Medium) for 45 seconds to 1½ minutes, or until roll is warm to the touch, rotating roll once during cooking time.

Total Cooking Time: ¾ to 1½ minutes

Variation:

Parmesan French Bread:
Follow the recipe for Cheese French Bread, except: Omit the cheese slice. In a small dish, microwave 2 tablespoons butter or margarine at High for 45 seconds to 1 minute, or until melted. Stir in 2 tablespoons of Parmesan cheese and, if desired, ⅛ teaspoon of garlic powder. Brush butter mixture between slits in French roll. Microwave as directed.

Bread Tips:
Paper towels absorb the moisture trapped between food and oven floor, and help keep bread surfaces dry.

Defrost loaf of bread by removing twist tie from bag and placing bread with wrapper in oven. Microwave at High for 45 seconds to 1¼ minutes, or until bread is cool but not icy. Let stand for 5 minutes to complete defrosting.

Warm breads and rolls by lining a nonmetallic basket with a cloth napkin, placing bread or rolls in basket and covering with a napkin. To warm: microwave six rolls at High for 15 seconds; ten rolls for 30 seconds; or one loaf (8 oz.) French bread for 30 seconds.

Herb-seasoned Croutons ▲

2 tablespoons butter or margarine
2 cups fresh bread cubes (½-inch cubes)
1 teaspoon dried parsley flakes
⅛ teaspoon poultry seasoning
⅛ teaspoon pepper

2 cups croutons

In a 9-inch square baking dish, microwave the butter at High for 45 seconds to 1 minute, or until melted. Add remaining ingredients; toss with a fork to coat bread cubes. Microwave at High for 4 to 7 minutes, or until bread is firm and dry to the touch, stirring after every minute of cooking time. Let stand to cool.

Total Cooking Time: 4¾ to 8 minutes

Variation:

Italian Seasoned Croutons:
Follow recipe for Herb-seasoned Croutons, except: substitute ⅛ teaspoon garlic powder for poultry seasoning; omit the pepper; add 2 teaspoons grated Parmesan cheese.

Ready-to-Go Honey Bran Muffins ▲

Ready-to-Go Muffins:
This muffin batter will keep in the refrigerator for up to one month. Mix up the batter, keep it on hand in the refrigerator, and you can have a hot muffin for breakfast or lunch in less than a minute — anytime you want.

1 cup boiling water
3 cups bran cereal
½ cup honey
½ cup packed brown sugar
½ cup sugar
½ cup shortening
2½ teaspoons baking soda
1 teaspoon salt
2 large eggs
2 cups buttermilk
2½ cups all-purpose flour

4 dozen muffins

1 Combine the water and cereal in a medium bowl; set aside. In a large bowl, beat together the honey, brown sugar, sugar, shortening, baking soda, salt and eggs. Stir in the buttermilk and soaked bran. Add flour; stir just until the mixture is combined.

2 Line custard cups or microwave cupcake dish with 2 paper liners each. Microwave at High as directed in chart (below). Refrigerate extra batter in an airtight container for up to 1 month.

Total Cooking Time: 20 seconds to 2½ minutes

Microwave at High:	Time:
1 muffin	20 seconds-1 minute
2 muffins	30 seconds-1½ minutes
3 muffins	1-2½ minutes

How to Microwave Muffins

Line each custard cup or microwave cupcake dish with 2 paper liners. When microwaving only 3 or 4 muffins in the cupcake dish, alternate cups for even baking.

7. Butter: Softens in Seconds, Melts in a Minute

Butter and margarine make good foods taste great. You can create new-tasting butters easily by softening them in the microwave to mix with other flavors. Explore how butter or margarine can be enhanced with the pungent punch of herbs, spices, wine, fruits and sweet or hot peppers. Special butters can give ordinary foods a touch of surprise.

Softening makes butter easy to spread or cream. To soften butter without melting it, microwave at 30% (Medium Low), checking every 15 seconds. To use as a spread, blend softened butter with minced herbs, onions or anchovies; serve with meats, fish or vegetables.

Melting butter is done quickly by microwaving at High. Melted butter can be blended with lemon juice, wine, or minced fresh herbs to create sauces for seafood or vegetables.

Microwave at High:	Time:
¼ cup butter	1¼-1½ minutes
½ cup butter	1½-1¾ minutes

Clarified Butter: Melt butter as directed in chart (above). The white foam which forms on the surface should be skimmed away immediately. Let butter stand for 1 to 2 minutes to allow any remaining solids to settle to the bottom. Spoon off the clear liquid to serve with fish and seafood. (White skimmed solids can be saved to toss with vegetables.)

Garlic Butter ▲

¼ cup water
2 cloves garlic, peeled
½ cup butter or margarine
2 tablespoons vegetable oil
1 teaspoon grated Parmesan cheese
⅛ teaspoon dry mustard

½ cup butter

1 In a 1-cup measure, microwave water and garlic at High for 1 minute, or until water boils. Set aside.

2 In a small bowl microwave the butter at 30% (Medium Low) for 15 seconds to 1 minute or just until softened, checking every 15 seconds.

3 Remove garlic from water; mash with fork. Add garlic to butter and blend in remaining ingredients. Beat with a fork until mixture is light and fluffy. Serve with meats, seafoods, hot cooked vegetables or breads.

Total Cooking Time: 1¼ to 2 minutes

Raspberry Butter ▲

½ cup butter or margarine
¾ cup powdered sugar
1 tablespoon raspberry jam

¾ cup butter

In a small bowl, microwave the butter at 30% (Medium Low) for 15 seconds to 1 minute or just until softened, checking every 15 seconds. Mix butter and sugar until smooth and creamy. Blend in the raspberry jam. Spread on toast, pancakes, waffles or quick breads.

Total Cooking Time: ¼ to 1 minute

Honey Butter

½ cup butter or margarine
⅓ cup honey

¾ cup butter

In a small bowl, microwave the butter at 30% (Medium Low) for 15 seconds to 1 minute or just until softened, checking every 15 seconds. Add honey and beat with an electric mixer until combined. Spread butter on toast, pancakes, waffles or quick breads.

Total Cooking Time: ¼ to 1 minute

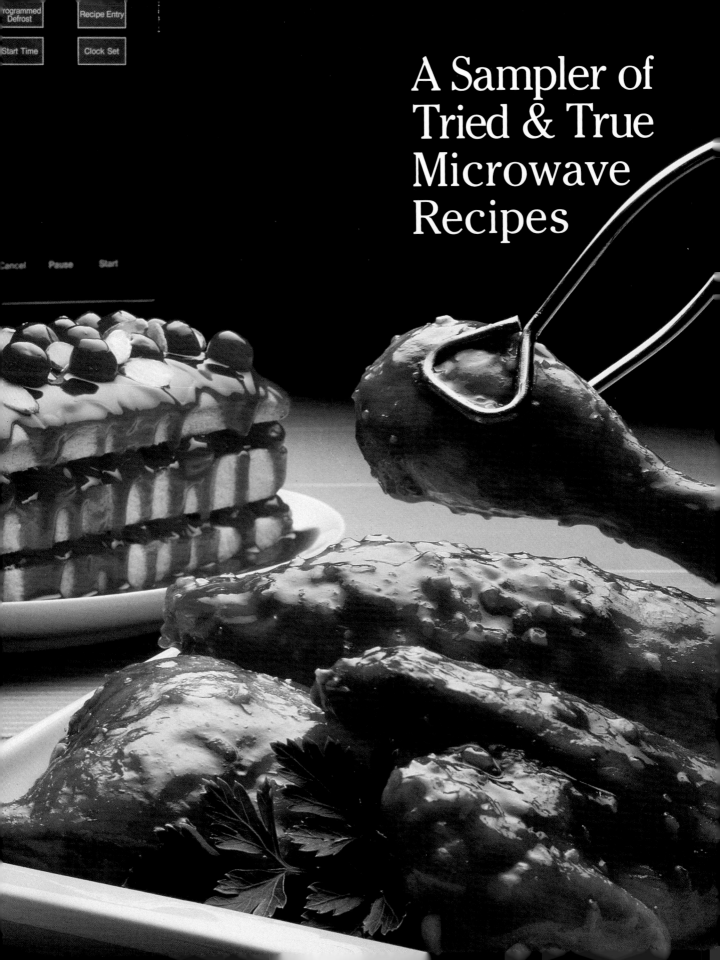

A Sampler of
Tried & True
Microwave
Recipes

Hot Snacks & Appetizers

A dozen spur-of-the-moment ideas —
Average cooking time: 5 minutes

Nachos

24 large tortilla chips
 1 cup shredded Monterey Jack, Cheddar or
      Colby cheese
¼ teaspoon chili powder
⅛ teaspoon ground cumin

4 servings

1 Arrange tortilla chips on a 10-inch plate. Place cheese in a plastic bag. Add the chili powder and cumin, shaking to coat cheese. Sprinkle mixture over chips.

2 Microwave at 50% (Medium) for 3 to 8 minutes, or until cheese melts, rotating dish 2 or 3 times during cooking.

Total Cooking Time: 3 to 8 minutes

Variations:

◄ Zippy Nachos:
Follow recipe for Nachos, except: sprinkle tortilla chips with sliced jalapeño peppers before microwaving.

Nachos with Salsa: ►
Follow recipe for Nachos, except: In a custard cup or small bowl, place ⅓ cup of salsa or taco sauce. Place custard cup in center of a 10-inch plate, then arrange tortilla chips on the plate. Sprinkle chips with the cheese mixture and microwave as directed.

Nachos with Beans:
Follow recipe for Nachos, except: spread tortilla chips with refried beans before sprinkling with cheese mixture. Top chips with 2 tablespoons chopped onion, and 2 tablespoons sliced black or green olives. If desired, sprinkle chips with shredded lettuce, chopped tomato and taco sauce before serving.

Pizza Crackers ▲

4 saltine crackers
  Prepared pizza sauce
1 slice (¾ oz.) mozzarella cheese, quartered
4 slices pepperoni

1 serving

Spread one side of each cracker with pizza sauce. Top each with a piece of cheese and a slice of pepperoni. Arrange crackers on a paper-towel-lined plate. Microwave at 50% (Medium) for 30 seconds to 1½ minutes, or until cheese melts, rotating dish 2 or 3 times during cooking.

Total Cooking Time: ½ to 1½ minutes

Hot Munchies ►

In a small bowl, combine the ingredients for the desired topping. Spread half the topping mixture on 12 melba toasts or other crackers. Arrange on a paper plate; microwave at High for 30 seconds to 1 minute, or until topping is heated, rotating once during cooking time. Repeat with remaining mixture and 12 more crackers. (If topping calls for softened cream cheese, microwave the cream cheese at High for 15 to 30 seconds.)

Total Cooking Time: ¾ to 1½ minutes

Midwest Bacon & Cheese (right)

4 slices bacon, cooked and crumbled
½ cup shredded Cheddar cheese
3 tablespoons mayonnaise
1 teaspoon dried parsley flakes
¼ teaspoon caraway seed (optional)

Seashore Crab (left)

1 pkg. (3 oz.) cream cheese, softened
1 can (6 oz.) crab meat, drained, rinsed, cartilage removed
½ teaspoon Worcestershire sauce
½ teaspoon lemon juice
2 tablespoons sliced green onion

Classic Ham 'n Cheese

1 can (4½ oz.) deviled ham spread
2 tablespoons finely chopped onion
¼ cup shredded Cheddar cheese
  Stuffed olives, sliced (optional)

Hawaiian Chicken (top)

1 pkg. (3 oz.) cream cheese, softened
1 can (5 oz.) chunk chicken, drained
2 tablespoons crushed pineapple
2 tablespoons chopped walnuts
2 tablespoons sliced green onion

Far-East Tuna (bottom)

1 can (3¼ oz.) tuna, drained
3 tablespoons mayonnaise
3 tablespoons finely chopped pecans
3 tablespoons drained, crushed pineapple
⅛ teaspoon curry powder

Crock Cheese

1 lb. Cheddar, Colby or Monterey Jack cheese
½ cup butter or margarine
1 pkg. (3 oz.) cream cheese
2 tablespoons finely chopped onion

1½ pounds cheese

Follow photo directions below.

Total Cooking Time: 2 to 8 minutes

Variations:

Port Wine Cheese:
Follow recipe for Crock Cheese, except: add ¼
cup of port wine, 2 tablespoons of snipped fresh
parsley, ¼ teaspoon of black pepper and ⅛
teaspoon of garlic powder to the Crock Cheese
mixture.

Pepper Cheese:
Follow recipe for Crock Cheese, except: add 1
tablespoon of chopped fresh or canned jalapeño
peppers, and ½ teaspoon of crushed red pepper
flakes to the Crock Cheese mixture.

How to Microwave Crock Cheese

1 Cut the cheese, butter and cream cheese into
1-inch pieces and place in a 2-quart casserole.
Microwave at 30% (Medium Low) for 2 to 8
minutes, or until cheese softens slightly, stirring
and rotating casserole after every minute of
cooking time. Watch carefully to avoid melting.

Cheese Ball or Log

1 recipe Crock Cheese (opposite)

Coatings:

1 cup finely chopped walnuts or pecans, plus ¼
    cup snipped fresh parsley

1 cup finely crushed corn chips

2 cheese balls or logs

1 Prepare Crock Cheese as directed (opposite), except do not pack mixture into dish.

2 Divide cheese mixture in half, and shape into two 3½-inch balls or two 6-inch logs.

3 Roll cheese in one of the coatings, and refrigerate for about 3 hours, or until firm. Serve with crackers or breadsticks.

Total Cooking Time: 2 to 8 minutes

Save Time Tomorrow:
Make two or more cheese balls. Use one now and freeze the rest. To serve, microwave at 30% (Medium Low) for 2 to 4 minutes. Let stand 10 to 15 minutes to complete defrosting.

2 Mash the cheese and butter pieces with a fork or pastry blender until the mixture is smooth.

3 Stir in the onion. Add any flavor variations desired (opposite). Pack mixture into serving dish; refrigerate until ready to serve.

Hot Crab Dip

1 pkg. (8 oz.) cream cheese
2 green onions, sliced
3 tablespoons mayonnaise
2 teaspoons lemon juice
1 teaspoon Worcestershire sauce
1 can (6 oz.) crab meat, drained, rinsed,
  cartilage removed

1½ cups

1 In a 1-quart serving dish, microwave the cream cheese at 50% (Medium) for 1½ to 3 minutes, or until it can be stirred smooth.

2 Blend in the onions, mayonnaise, lemon juice and Worcestershire sauce. Stir in crab meat.

3 Microwave at 50% (Medium) for 4 to 5 minutes, or until mixture is heated, stirring after every minute of cooking time. Serve with bread sticks, melba toasts or potato chips.

Total Cooking Time: 5½ to 8 minutes

Hot Dip Tip

Save cooking and cleanup time by substituting an ordinary casserole for special cooking utensils, such as chafing dishes, fondue pots, or hot plates. Return the dish to the microwave oven and reheat as often as needed.

Chili Con Queso Dip ▲

1 can (8 oz.) whole tomatoes, drained
1 can (4 oz.) chopped green chilies,
   drained
1 small onion, finely chopped
2 cups shredded Monterey Jack cheese
2 tablespoons all-purpose flour
⅓ cup whipping cream

About 2 cups

1 Combine the tomatoes, green chilies and
onion in a 1-quart casserole. Stir to break
apart tomatoes; cover. Microwave at High for 2
to 3 minutes, or until the onion is tender-crisp.

2 Place the shredded cheese and flour in a
plastic food-storage bag; shake to coat. Add
the coated cheese and whipping cream to
tomato mixture.

3 Microwave at 50% (Medium) for 1½ to 4
minutes, or until the cheese melts, stirring
twice during cooking time. Serve dip with
tortilla chips.

Total Cooking Time: 3½ to 7 minutes

Spinach Dip

1 pkg. (10 oz.) frozen chopped spinach
1 pkg. (8 oz.) cream cheese
¼ cup shredded carrot
2 tablespoons finely chopped onion
   Dash cayenne pepper
   Dash nutmeg

About 2 cups

1 Unwrap the frozen spinach; place on a plate.
Microwave at High for 4 to 6 minutes, or until
spinach is no longer icy. Let stand for 5 minutes.

2 In a 1½-quart casserole, microwave the cream
cheese at 50% (Medium) for 1½ to 3 minutes,
or until softened, stirring once or twice during
cooking time.

3 Drain the spinach, pressing to remove excess
moisture. Stir the spinach and remaining
ingredients into the cream cheese. Serve with
carrot and celery sticks.

Total Cooking Time: 5½ to 9 minutes

Ground Beef

From salads to meatloaf, the microwave cooks ground beef faster, with less cleanup

How to Microwave Ground Beef on Paper Towels

1 Speed cleanup by layering 4 paper towels in the bottom of a 2-quart casserole to absorb fat. Crumble 1 lb. of ground beef into casserole. Microwave at High for 4 to 7 minutes, or until meat is no longer pink, stirring gently to break apart 2 or 3 times during cooking.

2 Lift one side of the paper towels, allowing the ground beef to fall into the casserole. Discard paper towels, and continue with one of the following recipes.

Taco Salad

1 lb. ground beef, crumbled
1 medium onion, chopped
1 can (15 oz.) kidney beans, drained
½ cup water
1 pkg. (1¼ oz.) taco seasoning mix
½ medium head lettuce, torn into
    bite-size pieces
2 medium tomatoes, cut into chunks
½ cup shredded Cheddar cheese
½ cup shredded Monterey Jack cheese
1 cup broken corn chips

4 to 6 servings

1 Place the ground beef and onion in a 2-quart casserole; cover. Microwave at High for 4 to 7 minutes, or until the meat is no longer pink, stirring to break apart 2 or 3 times during cooking. Drain.

2 Add the kidney beans, water and seasoning mix. Microwave at 50% (Medium) for 10 to 13 minutes, or until the mixture thickens and bubbles, stirring once during cooking time.

3 In a large bowl, combine the lettuce and tomatoes. Spoon the meat mixture over the lettuce. Top with cheeses; sprinkle with corn chips. Serve with salsa or taco sauce.

Total Cooking Time: 14 to 20 minutes

Sloppy Joes ▲

1 lb. ground beef, crumbled
1 medium onion, chopped
1 can (10¾ oz.) condensed chicken
   gumbo soup
½ cup catsup
2 tablespoons packed brown sugar
2 teaspoons vinegar
2 teaspoons prepared mustard
½ teaspoon salt

4 to 6 servings

1 Place the ground beef and onion in a 2-quart casserole. Cover. Microwave at High for 4 to 7 minutes, or until the meat is no longer pink and the onion is tender, stirring to break meat apart 2 or 3 times during cooking. Drain.

2 Add the remaining ingredients. Microwave at High for 5 to 7 minutes, or until flavors are blended, stirring once during cooking time.

Total Cooking Time: 9 to 14 minutes

Spaghetti Sauce

1 lb. ground beef, crumbled
1 small onion, finely chopped
1 small carrot, shredded
⅛ teaspoon instant minced garlic
1 can (16 oz.) whole tomatoes
1 can (6 oz.) tomato paste
¾ cup dry red wine or beef broth
1 teaspoon salt
1 teaspoon Italian seasoning

About 2 quarts

1 In a 2-quart casserole, combine the ground beef, onion, carrot and garlic; cover. Microwave at High for 5 to 9 minutes, or until meat is no longer pink and the vegetables are tender, stirring 3 or 4 times during cooking. Drain.

2 Add the remaining ingredients, stirring to break apart tomatoes. Microwave at High for 5 minutes. Stir. Microwave at 50% (Medium) for 20 to 25 minutes longer, or until the flavors are blended, stirring once during cooking.

Total Cooking Time: 30 to 39 minutes

Creamy Hamburger Casserole

1 pkg. (3 oz.) cream cheese
1 lb. ground beef, crumbled
½ cup chopped onion
½ cup chopped celery
½ cup chopped green pepper
1 can (8 oz.) tomato sauce
2 cups uncooked egg noodles, prepared as
    directed on pkg.
½ cup cottage cheese
1 teaspoon salt
½ teaspoon dried basil leaves
1 medium tomato, sliced (optional)

4 servings

1 In a small bowl, microwave the cream cheese at High for 15 to 30 seconds, or until cheese is softened. Set aside.

2 In a 2-quart casserole, combine the ground beef, onion, celery and the green pepper; cover. Microwave at High for 4 to 6 minutes, or until meat is no longer pink and the vegetables are tender, stirring to break meat apart 2 or 3 times during cooking. Drain.

3 Stir in the tomato sauce, cooked noodles, cottage cheese, softened cream cheese, salt and basil. Microwave at High for 4 minutes. Stir.

4 Top casserole with tomato slices. Microwave at 50% (Medium) for 4 to 7 minutes, or until casserole is heated, rotating twice during cooking time.

Total Cooking Time: 12¼ to 17½ minutes

Versatile Tex-Mex Mix

2 lbs. ground beef, crumbled
½ cup chopped onion
¼ teaspoon instant minced garlic
1 tablespoon chili powder
¾ teaspoon salt
¾ teaspoon crushed red pepper flakes
¼ teaspoon ground cumin
⅛ teaspoon dried oregano leaves

4 containers

1 In a 3-quart casserole, mix the ground beef, onion, and garlic. Microwave at High for 6 to 10 minutes, or until the meat is no longer pink, stirring 2 or 3 times during cooking. Drain. Add remaining ingredients. Cover. Microwave at 50% (Medium) for 4 to 6 minutes longer, or until the flavors are blended, stirring once during cooking time. Divide into 4 equal portions. Use one portion immediately, or freeze all for future use.

2 *To defrost,* remove mix from one container and place in a 1-quart casserole. Microwave at 50% (Medium) for 1½ to 2 minutes, or until the mixture can be broken apart. Let stand for 5 to 10 minutes to complete defrosting. Use mix in Burritos, Tacos, or Mexican Pie recipes, opposite.

Total Cooking Time: 10 to 16 minutes

Burritos ▲

4 flour tortillas (8-inch diameter)
1 container Tex-Mex Mix, defrosted (left)
1 cup chopped tomato
1 cup shredded lettuce
1 medium avocado, mashed
¼ cup shredded Cheddar cheese

4 servings

1 Between damp paper towels, microwave tortillas at High for 30 seconds to 1 minute, or until warm to the touch. Place ¼ cup of the beef mix in the center of each tortilla. Spoon remaining ingredients, except cheese, equally onto tortillas. Fold one side over filling. Fold in adjoining sides, then remaining side.

2 Place burritos seam-side-down on a serving plate. Sprinkle with shredded Cheddar cheese. Microwave at 70% (Medium High) for 1½ to 3½ minutes, or until the cheese melts, rotating dish once during cooking time. If desired, serve with salsa sauce.

Total Cooking Time: 2 to 4½ minutes

Tacos ➤

1 container Tex-Mex Mix, defrosted (opposite)
8 taco shells
1 cup shredded Cheddar or Monterey Jack
   cheese

Toppings:
1 cup chopped tomato
⅓ cup chopped onion
1 cup shredded lettuce

4 servings

1 Place 2 tablespoons of the beef mix in each taco shell. Arrange the shells upright in a 9-inch square baking dish lined with paper towels. Sprinkle 2 tablespoons of cheese inside each taco shell.

2 Microwave at 70% (Medium High) for 1½ to 4 minutes, or until cheese melts, rotating dish once during cooking time. Sprinkle tacos with one or all of the toppings.

Total Cooking Time: 1½ to 4 minutes

Mexican Pie ➤

1 can (16 oz.) refried beans
1 baked pie shell (9-inch), cooled
1 cup shredded Cheddar cheese, divided
1 cup shredded Monterey Jack cheese, divided
1 container Tex-Mex Mix, defrosted (opposite)

Toppings:
1 cup shredded lettuce
½ cup chopped tomato
¼ cup sliced black olives
¼ cup chopped onion
¼ cup sour cream or salsa sauce

One 9-inch pie

1 Spread refried beans in the pie shell. Sprinkle ½ cup of the Cheddar cheese and ½ cup of the Monterey Jack cheese over the beans. Top with the Tex-Mex Mix and the remaining cheese.

2 Microwave at 50% (Medium) for 6 to 13 minutes, or until the cheese melts, rotating pie shell 3 or 4 times during cooking. Sprinkle pie with one or more of the toppings.

Total Cooking Time: 6 to 13 minutes

Basic Meatballs

1 lb. ground beef, crumbled
1 large egg
¼ cup chopped onion
¼ cup unseasoned dry bread crumbs
1 teaspoon dried basil, oregano leaves, or
   dried dill weed
½ teaspoon salt
½ teaspoon dry mustard
¼ teaspoon garlic powder
⅛ teaspoon pepper

             12 large or 20 small meatballs

Combine all ingredients in a medium bowl.
Shape the mixture into 12 large or 20 small
meatballs. Microwave as directed (below), or
until the meatballs are firm and no longer pink
in center.

Total Cooking Time: 6 to 10 minutes

Microwave at High:	Time:
12 large meatballs	6-9 minutes
20 small meatballs	8-10 minutes
12-20 saucy meatballs	6-10 minutes

Party Meatballs:
Prepare miniature meatballs as party
appetizers. Top the meatballs with 1 cup
prepared barbecue or sweet & sour sauce.
For easy clean-up, microwave and serve the
meatballs in the same dish. Serve with
decorative wooden toothpicks.

How to Microwave Basic Meatballs

1 Arrange meatballs in a 9-inch pie plate or
9-inch square baking dish. Microwave at High
as directed in chart (left).

2 Rotate large meatballs or rearrange small meatballs 3 or 4 times during cooking. If desired, serve with gravy.

Saucy Meatballs: Follow recipe for Basic Meatballs (opposite), except: pour off fat when rearranging meatballs, and add 1 can (8 oz.) tomato sauce, or 1 can (10¾ oz.) condensed mushroom soup, diluted with ¼ cup milk.

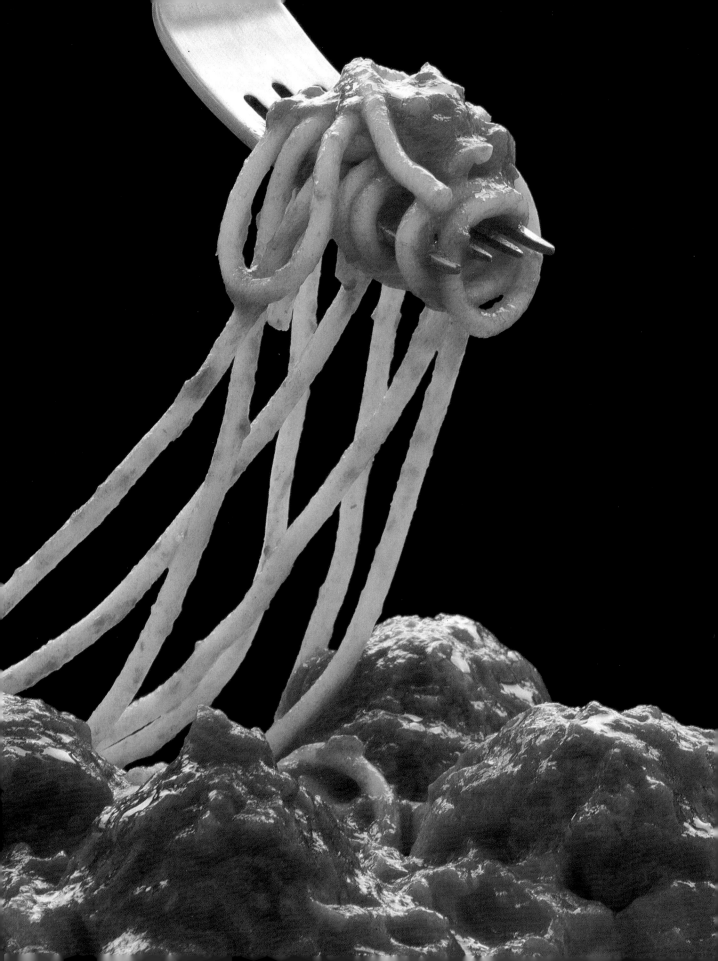

◄ Italian Meatballs

Meatballs:
1 recipe Basic Meatballs (page 52)
¼ cup chopped green pepper
¼ cup grated Parmesan cheese

Sauce:
1 can (16 oz.) tomato sauce
1 teaspoon dried parsley flakes
½ teaspoon Italian seasoning

20 meatballs

1 Prepare Basic Meatballs as directed, except omit the dry mustard, and add green pepper and Parmesan cheese to the meatball mixture. Shape mixture into 20 meatballs.

2 In a 2-quart casserole, microwave meatballs at High for 8 to 10 minutes, or until firm and no longer pink in center, stirring gently to rearrange 2 or 3 times during cooking. Drain.

3 Combine all the sauce ingredients; pour over meatballs. Microwave at High for 5 to 9 minutes, or until the sauce bubbles, stirring once during cooking time. Serve meatballs over hot cooked spaghetti.

Total Cooking Time: 13 to 19 minutes

Variation:

Pizza Meatballs:
Follow recipe for Italian Meatballs, except: add 1 can (6 oz.) tomato paste, ¼ cup sliced green olives, and ¼ teaspoon crushed red pepper flakes to the sauce mixture; sprinkle meatballs with 1 cup shredded mozzarella cheese during last two minutes of cooking.

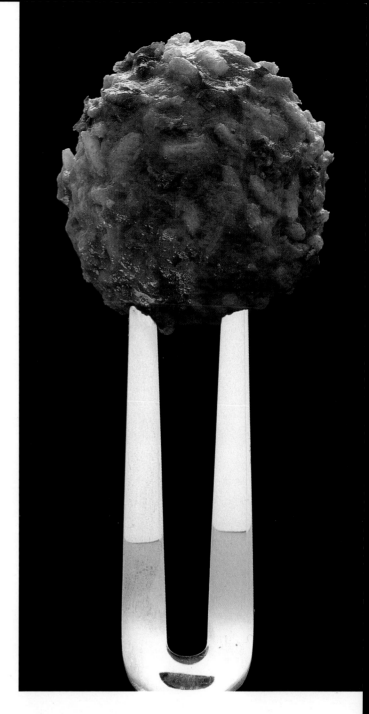

Porcupine Meatballs ▼

1 recipe Basic Meatballs (page 52)
1 cup uncooked instant rice
1 can (16 oz.) tomato sauce, divided
1½ teaspoons dried parsley flakes

4 servings

1 Prepare Basic Meatballs as directed, except: add rice, ½ cup of the tomato sauce and the dried parsley flakes to the meat mixture.

2 Shape the mixture into 12 meatballs; place in a 2-quart casserole. Top with the remaining tomato sauce; cover.

3 Microwave at High for 11 to 14 minutes, or until the meatballs are firm and no longer pink in the center, stirring gently to rearrange meatballs 3 or 4 times during cooking.

Total Cooking Time: 11 to 14 minutes

Basic Meatloaf

1½ lbs. ground beef, crumbled
1 large egg
¼ cup seasoned dry bread crumbs
¼ cup chopped onion
¼ cup chopped celery
1 tablespoon catsup
1½ teaspoons Worcestershire sauce
½ teaspoon salt
¼ teaspoon pepper

4 to 6 servings

1 Combine all the ingredients in a medium bowl. Shape the mixture into a loaf and place in an 8 × 4-inch loaf dish.

2 Microwave meatloaf at High for 13 to 18 minutes, or until meatloaf is firm, and temperature in the center is 145°F, rotating dish once during cooking time.

3 Let meatloaf stand, covered, for 5 minutes before serving.

Total Cooking Time: 13 to 18 minutes

How to Roll Meatloaf

Roll meatloaf, starting on short side. Lift paper until meat begins to roll tightly. Peel back paper to keep it free. Continue to lift and roll until meatloaf is completed.

◄ Italian Meatloaf

1 recipe Basic Meatloaf (above)
½ cup seasoned dry bread crumbs
1 can (8 oz.) tomato sauce, divided
1 cup shredded mozzarella cheese
1 teaspoon dried oregano leaves
2 tablespoons grated Parmesan cheese

4 to 6 servings

1 Prepare Basic Meatloaf mixture as directed, except: add the additional ½ cup seasoned dry bread crumbs and ½ cup of the tomato sauce to the mixture.

2 On wax paper, shape meatloaf mixture into a 12 × 8-inch rectangle, ½ inch thick. Sprinkle with mozzarella cheese.

3 Roll up loaf, starting on the short side. Lift the paper until the meat begins to roll tightly, enclosing the cheese. Continue to lift and peel back the paper while completing the roll. Seal edges of the finished roll.

4 Place the meatloaf in an 8 × 4-inch loaf dish, seam-side-down; cover with wax paper. Microwave at High for 10 minutes, rotating dish after half the cooking time. Microwave at 50% (Medium) for 14 to 20 minutes longer, or until loaf is firm and temperature in center is 145°F, rotating dish once during cooking time. Drain.

5 Combine the remaining tomato sauce and the oregano in a small bowl. Pour sauce over the meatloaf and sprinkle with Parmesan cheese. Microwave at 50% (Medium) for 2 minutes, or until the sauce is hot. Let stand for 5 minutes before serving.

Total Cooking Time: 26 to 32 minutes

◄ Savory Rolled Meatloaf

1 recipe Basic Meatloaf (page 57)
Filling:
¾ cup chopped green pepper
½ cup chopped onion
1 jar (2 oz.) diced pimiento, drained

4 to 6 servings

1 Prepare Basic Meatloaf mixture as directed. On wax paper, pat the meatloaf mixture into a 12 × 8-inch rectangle, ½ inch thick. Set aside.

2 Place the green pepper in a small bowl; cover. Microwave at High for 1½ to 2 minutes, or until the green pepper is tender-crisp. Sprinkle with green pepper, onion and pimiento, leaving a 1-inch border on all sides. Roll up the loaf (page 57), pressing the edges together to seal. Place meatloaf seam-side-down in an 8 × 4-inch loaf dish.

3 Microwave at High for 5 minutes. Microwave at 50% (Medium) for 20 to 30 minutes longer, or until meatloaf is firm and temperature in the center is 145°F, rotating the dish once during cooking time. Let stand, covered, for 5 minutes before serving.

Total Cooking Time: 26½ to 37 minutes

Miniature Meatloaf ▲

½ lb. ground beef, crumbled
1 slice soft white bread, crumbled
2 tablespoons milk
1 tablespoon chopped onion
2 tablespoons catsup, divided
1 teaspoon Worcestershire sauce
⅛ teaspoon garlic powder
⅛ teaspoon salt
⅛ teaspoon pepper
1 slice green pepper (optional)

1 to 2 servings

1 Place the ground beef in a medium bowl. Add the bread crumbs, milk, onion, 1 tablespoon of the catsup, Worcestershire sauce, garlic, salt and pepper.

2 Shape the mixture into a 3 × 5-inch loaf. Place loaf in a 9-inch pie plate. Microwave at High for 3 minutes.

3 Spread the remaining catsup over meatloaf. Top with green pepper slice. Microwave at High for 1 to 3½ minutes, or until the loaf is firm and temperature in center is 145°F. Let meatloaf stand for 2 minutes before serving.

Total Cooking Time: 4 to 6½ minutes

Chicken

Cook 4 pieces moist & tender in 12 minutes or less

Microwave at High:	Time:
¼ chicken (2 pieces)	6-9 minutes
½ chicken (4 pieces)	9-12 minutes

How to Microwave Chicken Pieces

1 Arrange chicken with meatiest parts to outside of dish. If desired, season with pinch of dried parsley flakes or tarragon leaves.

2 Cover tightly with plastic wrap vented at one edge of dish. Microwave for half of total cooking time listed in chart (above).

3 Rearrange chicken so that less-cooked areas are toward outside edge. Replace plastic wrap and microwave for remaining time, or until meat near bone is no longer pink and juices run clear.

Brush chicken pieces with barbecue sauce, soy sauce, or teriyaki sauce before microwaving, and when rearranging pieces, if desired.

Barbecue Chicken

2½ to 3-lb. whole broiler-fryer chicken, cut into
8 pieces, skin removed

Barbecue Sauce:
- ¾ cup chili sauce or catsup
- 3 tablespoons packed brown sugar
- 1 tablespoon vinegar or lemon juice
- 1 tablespoon minced dried onion
- 1 teaspoon prepared mustard
- 4 or 5 drops liquid smoke (optional)

4 servings

1 Arrange the chicken in a 9-inch square baking dish or a shallow 2-quart casserole. Cover with wax paper. Microwave chicken at High for 8 minutes, rearranging pieces once during cooking time. Drain.

2 Combine all the Barbecue Sauce ingredients in a 2-cup measure. Pour sauce over chicken pieces; re-cover with wax paper. Microwave at High for 5 to 10 minutes, or until meat near the bone is no longer pink, and the juices run clear, rearranging once during cooking time.

Total Cooking Time: 13 to 18 minutes

Lime-glazed Chicken ▲

- ½ cup water
- 2 tablespoons dark rum
- 2 tablespoons sugar
- 2 teaspoons cornstarch
- 1 teaspoon grated lime peel
- 1 teaspoon lime juice
- ¼ teaspoon instant chicken bouillon granules
- 2 tablespoons butter or margarine
- 1 teaspoon bouquet sauce
- 2 teaspoons water
- 2 whole bone-in chicken breasts (1½ to 2 lbs.)
  split into 4 breast halves, skin removed
- 4 thin slices lime

4 servings

1 In a 2-cup measure, combine ½ cup water, the rum, sugar, cornstarch, lime peel, lime juice and chicken bouillon. Add the butter.

2 Microwave at High for 1 to 2½ minutes, or until mixture is clear and thickened, stirring after each minute to melt the butter. Set aside. Combine the bouquet sauce and 2 teaspoons water in a small dish.

3 Arrange chicken bone-side-up in a 9-inch square baking dish, with meaty portions toward outside edges. Brush chicken with half the bouquet mixture. Cover with wax paper. Microwave at High for 5 minutes. Turn breasts over. Brush with the remaining bouquet sauce. Place 1 lime slice on each breast half. Re-cover. Microwave at High for 8 to 11 minutes longer, or until meat near the bone is no longer pink and the juices run clear. Serve with lime sauce.

Total Cooking Time: 14 to 18½ minutes

Chicken Breast Cacciatore ➤

1 can (16 oz.) whole tomatoes, cut up
½ medium green pepper, cut into thin strips
1 medium onion, sliced and separated
    into rings
¼ cup dry white wine
½ teaspoon dried parsley flakes
½ teaspoon sugar
½ teaspoon salt
¼ teaspoon dried oregano leaves
2 whole bone-in chicken breasts (1½ to 2 lbs.)
    split in 4 breast halves, skin removed
1 pkg. (7 oz.) uncooked vermicelli, prepared as
    directed on package
2 tablespoons grated Romano cheese

4 servings

1 In a 1-quart casserole, combine the tomatoes, green pepper, onion, wine and seasonings. Cover. Microwave at High for 5 to 8 minutes, or until the onion is tender-crisp, stirring once during cooking time.

2 Arrange chicken bone-side-up in a 9-inch square baking dish, with meaty portions toward outside edges. Pour tomato mixture over the chicken; cover with wax paper. Microwave at High for 5 minutes. Turn breasts over.

3 Microwave at High for 8 to 11 minutes longer, or until meat near the bone is no longer pink and juices run clear, rearranging the chicken once or twice during cooking time.

4 Toss vermicelli with Romano cheese. Serve chicken over vermicelli.

Total Cooking Time: 18 to 24 minutes

Cacciatore Tip:
If desired, cover chicken with plastic wrap, and while vermicelli cooks, prepare side dishes of Parmesan French Bread (page 31) and fresh cooked broccoli (page 79).

Fish

*Fish cooks moist, flaky & fast
in the microwave—
and defrosts in just minutes*

Defrosting tip:
*Use care in defrosting frozen fish. Separate
pieces as soon as you can; rearrange pieces
at half-time, and defrost only until they are
pliable, but still icy in the thick parts. Let fish
stand for 5 minutes to complete defrosting.*

Microwave at 70% (Med. High):	Time:
4 salmon steaks, ¾-inch thick (8 oz. each)	13-17 minutes

Microwave at High:	Time:
4 fish fillets, ½-inch thick (4 oz. each)	3-5 minutes

Allow 3 minutes standing time.

How to Microwave Poached Fish Fillets and Steaks

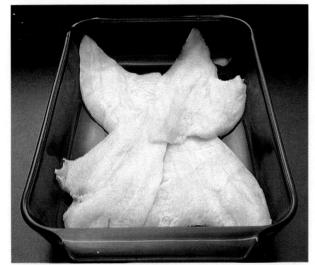

1 Arrange fillets with thickest portions towards outside. Overlap thin areas in center of dish. Sprinkle with lemon juice, melted butter or seasonings. Cover with vented plastic wrap. Microwave as directed in chart (above).

2 Move less-cooked portions to outside edges of dish after half the cooking time. Re-cover. Microwave for remainder of cooking time, or until fish flakes easily with a fork, rotating dish once or twice during cooking time.

Tangy Dill Topper

¼ cup mayonnaise
¼ cup plain yogurt
½ teaspoon lemon juice
¼ teaspoon dried dill weed
¼ teaspoon salt

½ cup

Combine all ingredients in a small bowl. Mix
thoroughly; chill. Use as a topping for hot
cooked fish fillets or steaks.

Seasoned Parsley Butter

¼ cup butter or margarine
2 teaspoons dried parsley flakes
   Dash garlic powder
   Dash salt
   Dash pepper

¼ cup

Combine all ingredients in a 1-cup measure.
Microwave at High for 1¼ to 1½ minutes,
or until the butter melts. Serve over hot cooked
fish fillets or steaks.

Total Cooking Time: 1¼ to 1½ minutes

◄ Fish with Piquant Topping

12 oz. fish fillets (½ inch thick) cut into
   4 serving-size pieces
1 can (16 oz.) stewed tomatoes, drained
2 tablespoons chili sauce
2 teaspoons red wine vinegar
½ teaspoon onion salt
¼ teaspoon dry mustard
⅛ teaspoon dried thyme leaves
⅛ teaspoon cayenne

4 servings

1 Arrange fish fillets in a 9-inch square baking
dish, with thickest portions toward outside
edges of dish. Set aside. Blend the remaining
ingredients in a small bowl. Spread mixture over
fillets; cover with plastic wrap.

2 Microwave at High for 5 to 10 minutes, or
until the fish flakes easily with a fork, rotating
dish once during cooking time. Let fish stand,
covered, for 3 minutes before serving.

Total Cooking Time: 5 to 10 minutes

Sunburst Fish Fillets ▲

12 oz. fish fillets (½ inch thick) cut into
   4 serving-size pieces
¼ cup dry vermouth
¼ to ½ teaspoon dried tarragon leaves
¼ teaspoon salt
½ medium orange, thinly sliced

4 servings

1 Arrange fillets in a 9-inch square baking dish,
with thickest portions toward outside edges of
dish. Pour vermouth over fillets, sprinkle with
tarragon and salt, and top with orange slices.
Cover with wax paper.

2 Microwave at High for 5 to 8 minutes, or until
fish flakes easily with a fork, rotating dish
once during cooking time. Let stand, covered,
for 3 minutes. Remove fish from cooking liquid
to serve.

Total Cooking Time: 5 to 8 minutes

Sandwiches

*From cold sandwich to
hot meal in 5 minutes*

Hot Deli Melt ➤

2 French rolls (3 oz. each) split lengthwise and
   toasted
1 recipe Poppy Seed Dressing (below) or
   mayonnaise
¼ lb. thinly sliced cooked beef, turkey or ham
½ cup alfalfa sprouts
4 thin slices tomato
⅓ cup sliced fresh mushrooms
4 thin slices onion
4 thin slices green pepper
2 slices (¾ oz. each) Cheddar, Colby or
   Swiss cheese

2 servings

1 Spread insides of French rolls with Poppy
  Seed Dressing. Layer the bottom half of each
roll with the meat, alfalfa sprouts, tomato slice,
mushrooms, onion, green pepper and cheese.
Add top half of roll.

2 Place both sandwiches on a paper-towel-lined
  plate. Microwave at 50% (Medium) for 3½ to
6½ minutes, or until the cheese is melted and
the bread is warm to the touch, rotating plate
once during cooking time.

Total Cooking Time: 3½ to 6½ minutes

Poppy Seed Dressing

¼ cup mayonnaise or salad dressing
¼ teaspoon prepared mustard
⅛ teaspoon poppy seed
   Dash garlic powder

¼ cup

Mix all dressing ingredients in a small bowl.
Use for Hot Deli Melt (above) or for other
sandwiches.

*Defrost and Warm Frozen Bagels:
Wrap bagels in a napkin and microwave at
High; 15 to 30 seconds for one bagel; 30 to 45
seconds for two.*

Canadian Bagel

2 tablespoons (1 oz.) cream cheese with chives
1 plain bagel, split and toasted
2 slices fully cooked Canadian bacon
2 tablespoons shredded Cheddar cheese

1 serving

1 In a small bowl, microwave the cream cheese at High for 10 to 20 seconds, or until softened.

Spread cream cheese on bottom half of bagel. Top with the Canadian bacon and the cheese.

2 Replace the bagel top. Wrap bagel in a paper towel; microwave at 50% (Medium) for 30 seconds to 1 minute, or until the bagel is warm to the touch.

Total Cooking Time: ½ to 1½ minutes

Toastwiches

2 slices toasted bread (white, wheat or rye)
Combination of the following:
Meat:
2 oz. sliced fully cooked meat (turkey, beef,
    ham or salami)
Vegetables:
  Sliced tomatoes
  Fresh alfalfa sprouts
  Cucumber slices
  Onion slices
  Green onion slices
  Radish slices
  Green pepper slices
Cheese:
  Assorted cheese slices (Cheddar, American,
    Colby, Swiss, brick)
Condiments:
  Butter or margarine
  Mayonnaise or salad dressing
  Prepared mustard
  Catsup
  Sour cream

1 serving

1 Top one slice of toast with the meat of your
choice. Add vegetables as desired; top with a
cheese slice. Place toast on a paper-towel-lined
serving plate.

2 Microwave at High for 30 seconds to 1¼
minutes, or until the cheese melts. Spread the
remaining slice of toast with a condiment of
your choice. Place on top of cheese to complete
the sandwich.

Total Cooking Time: ½ to 1¼ minutes

When Heating Sandwiches:
Always place them on a paper-towel-lined
plate, or wrap them in a paper towel, to
prevent sandwiches from becoming soggy.

Lamb Pocket Sandwiches ➤

½ lb. ground lamb, crumbled
1 slice bacon, finely chopped
¼ cup sliced green onion
¼ teaspoon dried mint leaves
¼ teaspoon salt
⅛ teaspoon instant minced garlic
⅛ teaspoon pepper
1 medium tomato, chopped
¼ cup chopped cucumber
¼ cup snipped fresh parsley
2 pita loaves (5-inch diameter)

2 servings

1 Place the lamb in a 1½-quart casserole. Add the bacon, green onion, mint, salt, garlic and pepper. Cover with a paper towel.

2 Microwave at High for 2 to 4 minutes, or until the meat is no longer pink, stirring to break lamb apart once during cooking time. Drain.

3 Stir in the tomato, cucumber and parsley. Slice pita loaves in half to form pockets. Spoon filling into pockets.

Total Cooking Time: 2 to 4 minutes

Individual Pizzas

3 English muffins, split and toasted
6 tablespoons prepared pizza sauce
18 thin slices pepperoni
¼ cup sliced mushrooms
¾ cup shredded mozzarella cheese, divided

6 individual pizzas

1 Spread each muffin half with 1 tablespoon of the pizza sauce. Top each muffin with 3 slices of pepperoni, a few of the mushroom slices, and 1 tablespoon of the mozzarella cheese.

2 Arrange muffin halves on a paper-towel-lined plate. (If desired, sprinkle pizzas with grated Parmesan cheese, chopped onion, and chopped black or green olives.) Microwave at High for 1½ to 3½ minutes, or until the cheese melts, rotating the plate once during cooking time.

Total Cooking Time: 1½ to 3½ minutes

Soups & Sauces

*Heat-and-serve easy,
one-dish cleanup*

◄ French Onion Soup

3 or 4 medium onions, thinly sliced
¼ cup butter or margarine
1 can (10¾ oz.) condensed chicken broth
1 can (10¾ oz.) condensed beef broth
  Hot tap water
4 slices French bread, toasted
2 cups shredded Swiss cheese
¼ cup grated Parmesan cheese

4 servings

1 Place onions and butter in a 2-quart casserole. Cover. Microwave at High for 6 to 8 minutes, or until the onion is tender, stirring once during cooking time.

2 Combine chicken and beef broth in a 4-cup measure. Add enough hot water to equal 4 cups. Add the broth mixture to the onions. Cover. Microwave at High for 4 to 6 minutes, or until mixture is hot. Ladle soup into 4 soup bowls.

3 Top each serving with one French bread slice and ¼ of each variety of cheese. Arrange bowls in oven. Microwave at High for 5½ to 7½ minutes, or until the cheese melts. (For smaller ovens, heat 2 bowls at a time at High for 2¾ to 3¾ minutes.)

Total Cooking Time: 15½ to 21½ minutes

WATER-BASED SOUPS (dilute as directed)	
Microwave at High:	**Time:**
1 serving (1½ cups)	2-3 minutes
2 servings (2-3½ cups)	3-5 minutes

MILK-BASED SOUPS (dilute as directed)	
Microwave at 50% (Medium):	**Time:**
1 serving (1½ cups)	3-5 minutes
2 servings (2-3½ cups)	6-12 minutes

Beer Cheese Soup ▲

¼ cup butter or margarine
½ cup all-purpose flour
2 tablespoons instant onion flakes
1 can (12 oz.) evaporated milk
1 cup milk
1 jar (16 oz.) pasteurized process cheese spread
1 can (12 oz.) beer

6 servings

1 In a 3-quart casserole, microwave butter at High for 1¼ to 1½ minutes, or until butter melts. Blend in the flour and onion flakes. Add the evaporated milk and the milk, ⅓ at a time, blending after each addition.

2 Microwave at High for 5 to 7½ minutes, or until mixture thickens and bubbles, stirring 2 or 3 times during cooking. Stir in the cheese until the mixture is smooth and the cheese is melted. Blend in the beer.

3 Microwave at High for 2 to 6 minutes, or until soup reaches desired serving temperature. If desired, garnish each serving with popcorn or pretzels.

Total Cooking Time: 8¼ to 15 minutes

Garden Vegetable Soup ▲

1 can (10¾ oz.) condensed chicken broth
1 can (10¾ oz.) hot tap water
1 teaspoon soy sauce
½ teaspoon sugar
⅛ teaspoon dried thyme leaves
⅛ teaspoon dried basil leaves
⅛ teaspoon onion powder (optional)
2 teaspoons cornstarch
¼ lb. fresh broccoli
1 medium carrot, cut into thin strips
1 cup shredded lettuce

2 servings

1 In a 2-quart casserole, combine the chicken broth, hot water, soy sauce, sugar, thyme, basil and onion powder. Blend the cornstarch into a small amount of the broth; stir cornstarch mixture back into broth. Microwave at High for 6 to 11 minutes, or just until mixture boils.

2 Cut broccoli stems into thin slices and cut the flowerets into small pieces. Add broccoli and carrot to boiling broth; cover. Microwave at High for 2 to 5 minutes, or until vegetables are tender-crisp. Stir in the shredded lettuce. Let stand, covered, for 5 minutes before serving.

Total Cooking Time: 8 to 16 minutes

Split Pea Soup

¼ cup thinly sliced celery
¼ cup thinly sliced carrot
¼ cup finely chopped onion
¼ cup finely chopped bacon or ham
1 can (11¼ oz.) condensed split pea soup
1¼ cups milk
⅛ teaspoon dried thyme leaves

4 to 6 servings

1 In a 1½-quart casserole, combine the celery, carrot, onion and bacon. Cover. Microwave at High for 4 to 5 minutes, or until the vegetables are tender, stirring once during cooking time.

2 Add the remaining ingredients. Re-cover. Microwave at High for 5 to 6 minutes, or until soup reaches the desired serving temperature, stirring 2 or 3 times during cooking.

Total Cooking Time: 9 to 11 minutes

Soup Toppings Tip:
To give soups an added crunch, sprinkle before serving with one of the following: pretzels, plain or cheese popcorn or oyster crackers.

Cream of Broccoli Soup

  1 pkg. (10 oz.) frozen broccoli cuts
  1 can (10¾ oz.) condensed cream of
     mushroom soup
1½ cups milk
  1 teaspoon freeze-dried chives
⅛ teaspoon pepper
     Dash nutmeg

4 servings

1 Unwrap the broccoli and place on a plate. Microwave at High for 4 to 6 minutes, or until defrosted; turning over and breaking apart once during cooking time. Drain broccoli and chop into fine pieces. Place broccoli in a 2-quart casserole and add remaining ingredients; cover.

2 Microwave at High for 6 to 12 minutes, or until soup reaches desired serving temperature, stirring 2 or 3 times during cooking. If desired, top servings with sour cream.

Total Cooking Time: 9 to 17 minutes

Menu Tip:
Serve Cream of Broccoli Soup as an accompaniment with Canadian Bagel Sandwich (page 69).

Serve Cream of Broccoli Soup as an accompaniment with Canadian Bagel Sandwich (page 69).

Soup Tip:
When microwaving canned soups, use High power for water-added soups, and 50% (Medium) power for those which use milk. You can also spruce up soups with added vegetables, cheese, herbs, spices, toppings and even other soups.

New Soups From Two Soups

In a 2-quart casserole, dilute one of the soup combinations (below) with 2 cans of liquid (use hot water, milk or a combination of both: For a richer, creamier soup, dilute with 1 can of milk and 1 can of half-and-half; or use 1 can (12 oz.) of evaporated milk and ¼ cup of hot water). For extra zest, stir in 1 tablespoon of dried onion flakes or 1 to 2 teaspoons of dried chives. If desired, add salt and pepper.

Microwave, covered, at High for 5 to 9 minutes, or until the soup reaches the desired serving temperature. Stir 2 or 3 times during cooking.

Clam & Potato Chowder
  1 can (10¾ oz.) condensed New England
     clam chowder
  1 can (10¾ oz.) condensed cream of potato
     soup

Creamy Chicken Vegetable Soup
  1 can (10¾ oz.) condensed cream of chicken
     soup
  1 can (10¾ oz.) condensed chicken vegetable
     soup

Bean, Pea & Pork Soup
  1 can (11¼ oz.) condensed split-pea-with-ham
     soup
  1 can (11½ oz.) condensed bean-with-bacon
     soup

Hearty Chowder
  1 can (10¾ oz.) condensed New England
     clam chowder
  1 can (10¾ oz.) condensed tomato soup

DRY SAUCE MIXES (¾-1¾ oz.)

Microwave at High:	Time:
Mix calls for:	
⅔-1 cup water	1-3 minutes
1¼ cup water	3-5 minutes
1 cup milk	2½-5 minutes
1¼ cups milk	4-6 minutes
2¼ cups milk	6-9 minutes

Stir 2 or 3 times during cooking time.

Basic White Sauce

2 tablespoons butter or margarine
2 tablespoons all-purpose flour
¼ teaspoon salt
⅛ teaspoon pepper
1 cup milk

About 1 cup

In a 4-cup measure, microwave the butter at High for 45 seconds to 1 minute, or until melted. Stir in the flour, salt and pepper until mixture is smooth. Blend in the milk. Microwave at High for 3½ to 5 minutes, or until mixture thickens and bubbles, stirring well once or twice during cooking time.

Total Cooking Time: 4 to 6 minutes

Variations:

Cheese Sauce:
Follow recipe for Basic White Sauce, except: add ½ cup of shredded cheese after sauce thickens and bubbles. Stir to melt.

◄ Mornay Sauce:
Follow recipe for Basic White Sauce, except: add ¼ cup shredded Swiss cheese, 2 tablespoons grated Parmesan cheese and 1 teaspoon dried parsley flakes after sauce thickens and bubbles. Stir to melt.

Easy Bearnaise Sauce ▲

3 egg yolks
2 teaspoons white wine
¼ teaspoon dried tarragon leaves
¼ teaspoon salt
½ cup butter or margarine
1 tablespoon minced onion

¾ cup

1 In a food processor or blender bowl, combine the egg yolks, wine, tarragon and salt. Process for about 5 seconds, or until mixture is smooth.

2 Place the butter and onion in a 2-cup measure. Microwave at High for 1¾ to 2¼ minutes, or until the butter melts and bubbles. Continue to blend egg yolks at low speed; add the hot butter and onion mixture in a slow and steady stream until the sauce thickens. Serve immediately with fish or beef.

Total Cooking Time: 1½ to 2½ minutes

Vegetables

Microwaving helps retain the flavor, vitamins and minerals of fresh vegetables

◄ ## Vegetable Butter Topping

3 tablespoons butter or margarine
1 tablespoon snipped fresh parsley
½ teaspoon freeze-dried chives
¼ teaspoon salt
⅛ teaspoon pepper
2 teaspoons grated Parmesan cheese

About ¼ cup

In a 1-cup measure, combine the butter, parsley, chives, salt and pepper. Microwave at High for 1 to 1¼ minutes, or until the butter melts. Stir in the Parmesan cheese. Serve topping over hot cooked vegetables.

Total Cooking Time: 1 to 1¼ minutes

Variations:

Vegetables Almondine Butter:
Follow recipe for Vegetable Butter Topping, except: omit parsley and Parmesan cheese; stir 1 tablespoon of sliced almonds and a dash of garlic powder into the melted butter.

Lemony Vegetable Butter:
Follow recipe for Vegetable Butter Topping, except: omit parsley and Parmesan cheese; stir 1 tablespoon sliced pimiento, 1 teaspoon lemon juice and ¼ teaspoon dried basil leaves into the melted butter.

Herb Butter Topping:
Follow recipe for Vegetable Butter Topping, except: omit chives and Parmesan cheese; stir ⅛ teaspoon dried marjoram leaves and a dash of dried thyme leaves into the melted butter.

Microwave at High:		Time:
Asparagus	1 lb.	7-10 minutes

Trim. Cut into 1-inch pieces. Place in 2-qt. casserole with ¼ cup water. Cover. Microwave, stirring once. Let stand 3 minutes. Drain.

Broccoli	1 lb.	8-12 minutes

Trim. Cut into 1-inch pieces. Place in 2-qt. casserole with ¼ cup water. Cover. Microwave, stirring once. Let stand 3 minutes. Drain.

Carrots	2 cups, sliced	4-8 minutes

Place in 1-qt. casserole with 2 tablespoons water. Cover. Microwave, stirring once. Let stand 3 minutes. Drain.

Cauliflower	1 med. head	7-10 minutes

Trim for flowerettes. Place in 1½-qt. casserole with ¼ cup water. Cover. Microwave, stirring once. Let stand 5 minutes. Drain.

Corn	2 med. ears	5-10 minutes
	4 med. ears	8-16 minutes

Remove husk. Rinse. Wrap each ear with plastic wrap. Microwave, rearranging once. Let stand 5 minutes.

Green Beans	1 lb.	12½-17½ minutes

Trim. Cut into 1½-inch pieces. Place in 1½-qt. casserole with ½ cup water. Cover. Microwave, stirring once. Let stand 5 minutes. Drain.

Spinach	1 lb.	6-9 minutes

Wash. Trim. Place in 2-qt. casserole with ¼ cup water. Cover. Microwave, stirring once. Let stand 3 minutes. Drain.

Frozen Vegetables

Frozen Vegetable Dress-Ups

To 1 pkg. (10 oz.) frozen chopped spinach: Add ½ cup sliced water chestnuts and ½ cup fresh bean sprouts. Microwave according to chart (opposite).

To 1 pkg. (10 oz.) frozen asparagus: Add ½ teaspoon grated orange peel. Microwave according to chart (opposite). Top with ¼ cup toasted almonds before serving.

To 1 pkg. (10 oz.) frozen corn: Add 1 tablespoon finely chopped onion, 1 tablespoon chopped pimiento and 1 tablespoon fresh snipped parsley. Microwave according to chart (opposite).

To 1 pkg. (10 oz.) frozen peas: Add ½ cup sliced mushrooms and 1 tablespoon sliced green onion. Microwave according to chart (opposite).

To 1 pkg. (10 oz.) frozen cauliflower: Microwave according to chart (opposite); top with ⅓ cup shredded Cheddar cheese and 1 tablespoon sunflower nuts.

To 1 pkg. (9 oz.) frozen French-style green beans: Add ½ teaspoon grated lemon peel and ⅓ cup sliced almonds. Microwave according to chart (opposite).

To 1 pkg. (10 oz.) frozen chopped broccoli: Add 1 tablespoon vegetable oil and ⅛ to ¼ teaspoon crushed red pepper flakes. Microwave according to chart (opposite).

To 1 pkg. (10 oz.) frozen mixed vegetables: Add 2 tablespoons butter or margarine and ½ teaspoon dried thyme leaves. Microwave according to chart (opposite).

To 1 pkg. (10 oz.) frozen Brussel sprouts: Microwave according to chart (opposite); top with ¼ cup toasted chopped walnuts or pecans.

Cheesy Green Beans Almondine

2 pkgs. (9 oz. each) frozen French-style green beans
1 can (4 oz.) sliced mushrooms, drained
1 pkg. (8 oz.) pasteurized process cheese spread loaf, cut into ½-inch cubes
2 tablespoons sliced almonds

4 to 6 servings

1 Place the green beans in a 1½-quart casserole. Cover; microwave at High for 8 to 10 minutes, or until beans are tender, stirring to break apart once during cooking time. Drain.

2 Add the mushrooms and cheese. Re-cover. Microwave at High for 2 to 5 minutes, or until the cheese melts, stirring once during cooking time. Sprinkle with almonds before serving.

Total Cooking Time: 10 to 15 minutes

Broccoli Butter Toss

1 pkg. (10 oz.) frozen chopped broccoli (or 3
   cups fresh broccoli flowerets)
2 medium carrots, cut into thin strips
2 tablespoons water
2 tablespoons butter or margarine
1 tablespoon snipped fresh parsley
¼ teaspoon salt
⅛ teaspoon pepper

4 servings

1 In a 1-quart casserole, combine the broccoli,
carrots and water. Cover. Microwave at High
for 5½ to 7 minutes, or until the vegetables are
tender-crisp, stirring once during cooking time.
Drain vegetables.

2 In a 6-oz. custard cup, combine the remaining
ingredients. Microwave at High for 45 seconds
to 1 minute, or until the butter melts. Pour the
mixture over broccoli and carrots; toss to coat.

Total Cooking Time: 6¼ to 8 minutes

Microwave at High:		Time:
Asparagus (10-oz. pkg.)	Place in 1-qt. casserole with 2 tablespoons water. Cover. Microwave, stirring once. Let stand 3 minutes. Drain.	7-9 minutes
Beans — Green, Waxed or Lima (9-oz. pkg.)	Prepare as above	5-8 minutes
Broccoli (10-oz. pkg.)	Prepare as above.	7-10 minutes
Brussels Sprouts (10-oz. pkg.)	Prepare as above.	6-8 minutes
Cauliflower (10 oz. pkg.)	Prepare as above.	5-8 minutes
Corn (10-oz. pkg.)	Prepare as above.	5-7 minutes
Peas (10-oz. pkg.)	Prepare as above.	6-8 minutes
Spinach (10-oz. pkg.)	Prepare as above.	5-8 minutes
Squash, mashed (10-oz. pkg.)	Prepare as above, except add no water.	6-8 minutes
Mixed, Vegetables (10-oz. pkg.)	Prepare as above.	5-7 minutes

Portioning Tip:
*One 9 or 10 oz. package of frozen vegetables
is equal to about 2 cups.*

Rice & Cereals

*Perfect results every time,
and easy cleanup, too*

Microwave Method for Rice:	Time:
Long-grain, converted	
Combine 1 cup uncooked converted rice, 2¼ cups water in 2-qt. casserole. Cover. Microwave. Let stand, covered, 5 minutes.	5 min. at High, 15-22 min. at 50% (Med.)
Long-grain, white	
Combine 1 cup uncooked long-grain rice, 2 cups water in 2-qt. casserole. Cover. Microwave. Let stand, covered, 5 minutes.	5 min. at High, 12-15 min. at 50% (Med.)

Vegetable Rice Mix

  1 medium carrot, finely chopped
  ¼ cup chopped green pepper
  2 tablespoons chopped onion
  2 tablespoons butter or margarine
  1 can (4 oz.) sliced mushrooms, drained
1½ cups uncooked instant rice
1¼ cups chicken broth
  ½ teaspoon salt
  ⅛ teaspoon pepper

4 servings

1 In a 2-quart casserole, combine the carrot, green pepper, onion and butter. Cover. Microwave at High for 4 to 8 minutes, or until the vegetables are tender, stirring once during cooking time.

2 Add the mushrooms, rice, chicken broth, salt and pepper. Re-cover. Microwave at High for 5 to 7 minutes, or until the liquid is absorbed, stirring once during cooking time. Let stand, covered, for 5 minutes.

Total Cooking Time: 9 to 15 minutes

Variation:

▲ Curry Rice:
Follow recipe for Vegetable Rice Mix, except: Add ½ cup chopped apple, ¼ cup raisins, ¼ cup cashews and 1 teaspoon curry powder to the vegetables and melted butter. Continue as directed.

Shrimp & Rice

1⅔ cups water
1 pkg. (4.6 oz.) chicken-flavored rice and
    sauce mix
2 tablespoons chopped red or green pepper
2 tablespoons chopped onion
1 tablespoon butter or margarine
¼ lb. small shrimp uncooked, peeled and
    deveined

4 servings

1 In a 1½-quart casserole, combine all the
ingredients, except the shrimp. Cover.
Microwave at High for 10 to 13 minutes, or
until the rice is tender, stirring once during
cooking time.

2 Stir in the shrimp. Re-cover. Microwave at 50%
(Medium) for 2 to 3 minutes, or until shrimp
are opaque, stirring once during cooking time.
Let stand, covered, for 3 minutes.

Total Cooking Time: 12 to 16 minutes

Rice Medley

1 cup uncooked long-grain rice
¼ cup chopped green or red pepper
2 tablespoons snipped fresh parsley
1 tablespoon finely chopped celery
2¼ cups hot tap water
2 tablespoons white wine
½ teaspoon salt
¼ teaspoon bouquet garni seasoning

4 to 6 servings

1 Combine all the ingredients in a 2-quart
casserole. Cover. Microwave at High for
5 minutes.

2 Microwave at 50% (Medium) for 15 to 22
minutes longer, or until the liquid is absorbed
and the rice is tender. Let stand, covered, for 5
minutes. Toss lightly.

Total Cooking Time: 20 to 27 minutes

Wild Rice Medley ▲

2 tablespoons butter or margarine
¼ cup slivered almonds
¼ cup chopped onion
¼ cup chopped celery
1 can (4 oz.) sliced mushrooms, drained
½ teaspoon salt
¼ teaspoon dried thyme leaves
⅛ teaspoon pepper
3 cups cooked wild rice

4 to 6 servings

1 Combine the butter and almonds in a 2-quart
casserole. Microwave at High for 3½ to
4 minutes, or until the almonds are lightly
browned. Add the onion, celery, mushrooms,
salt, thyme and pepper. Cover.

2 Microwave at High for 2 to 4 minutes longer,
or until the vegetables are tender. Add the
rice; stir to combine. Cover. Microwave at High
for 1½ to 3 minutes longer, or until the mixture
is heated.

Total Cooking Time: 7 to 11 minutes

Microwave Method for Cereals:		Time:
Oats, Old-fashioned:		
Combine ⅔ cup oats, 1⅓ cups water in 1½-qt. casserole.	Microwave, uncovered, until cereal is desired consistency, stirring 2 or 3 times.	5-7 minutes
Oats, Quick-cooking:		
Combine ⅔ cup oats, 1½ cups water in 1½-qt. casserole.	prepare as above	4-6 minutes
Cream of Wheat®, Regular:		
Combine ⅓ cup cereal, 1¾ cups water in 2-qt. casserole.	prepare as above	6-8 minutes
Quick-cooking:		
Combine ⅓ cup cereal, 1⅓ cups water in 2-qt. casserole	prepare as above	2½-4 minutes

◄ Spiced Creamy Cereal

2 cups milk
⅓ cup regular uncooked cream of wheat cereal
2 tablespoons chopped dried apricots
⅛ teaspoon salt
  Dash ground nutmeg
  Dash ground allspice

2 servings

Combine all ingredients in a 2-quart casserole. Microwave at High for 6 to 8 minutes, or until the cereal thickens, stirring 2 or 3 times during cooking.

Total Cooking Time: 6 to 8 minutes

Cereal Tip:
Microwave cereals are quick to prepare and wholesome to eat. You can microwave individual servings, but use a large enough bowl to allow the cereal to cook without boiling over.

Sunny Couscous Cereal ▲

¾ cup water
¼ cup orange juice or apple juice
½ cup uncooked couscous
1 teaspoon grated orange peel
2 tablespoons finely chopped blanched almonds
1 tablespoon honey
  Dash ground cinnamon

4 servings

Combine all ingredients in a 1-quart casserole. Cover. Microwave at High for 5 to 6 minutes, or until the liquid is absorbed and couscous is tender. Let stand, covered, for 1 minute.

Total Cooking Time: 5 to 6 minutes

Desserts

Simple & delicious: now you <u>do</u> have time to make dessert

◄ Cherry Almond Torte

1 can (21 oz.) cherry pie filling
2 teaspoons almond extract (or ¼ cup
　　Amaretto)
1 frozen pound cake (10 ¾ oz.) sliced
　　lengthwise into thirds
3 tablespoons sliced almonds

　　　　　　　　　　　　　6 to 8 servings

Combine the pie filling and almond extract in a medium bowl. Place the bottom ⅓ of the pound cake on a serving plate. Spoon ⅓ of the fruit mixture onto the cake, then sprinkle with 1 tablespoon of the sliced almonds. Repeat with the remaining layers. Microwave at High for 2 to 4 minutes, or until heated, rotating 2 or 3 times during cooking.

　　Total Cooking Time: 2 to 4 minutes

Variation:

Strawberry & Cream Torte:
Follow recipe for Cherry Almond Torte, except: Slice the pound cake as directed. Slice 1 cup of fresh strawberries; set aside. In a medium bowl, microwave 1 pkg. (8 oz.) of cream cheese at 50% (Medium) for 1½ to 3 minutes, or until cream cheese is softened. Stir in ½ cup of prepared whipped topping, ½ teaspoon grated lemon peel and 3 tablespoons of powdered sugar. Place the bottom ⅓ of the pound cake on a serving plate; spread with a thin layer of the cream cheese mixture. Top with ⅓ of the strawberries. Repeat with the remaining layers. Frost the sides and top with remaining cream cheese mixture. Garnish with remaining strawberries.

Pudding, Pie Filling & Gelatin

Place pudding mix in a 1½-quart casserole or 4-cup measure. Blend in milk and the other ingredients as directed on package. Microwave at High as directed in chart (below), or until the mixture thickens or boils, stirring every 2 minutes. Cool. Use pudding mix to fill prepared pie crust, or layer in parfait glasses with whipped cream and chopped nuts.

For gelatin, boil water in microwave. Prepare as directed on package. Stir in fresh or canned fruit, nuts or marshmallows when gelatin is soft-set; refrigerate until firm.

Microwave at High:		Time:
Pudding and Pie Filling		
1½-4⅛ oz. package	Mix as directed above.	6-9 minutes, stirring every 2 minutes.
4½-6⅛ oz. package	Use 2-qt. casserole. Mix as directed above.	7-10 minutes, stirring after 3 minutes, then every 2 minutes.
Gelatin Mixes		
0.3-6 oz. package	Follow package directions. Boil water in microwave.	1 cup: 2-3 minutes 2 cups: 4-5 minutes

◄ Chocolate-dipped Strawberries

Coating:
½ lb. chocolate candy coating
1 tablespoon shortening
Dipper:
1 quart strawberries, washed

1 quart

1 Combine coating ingredients in a 2-cup measure. Microwave at 50% (Medium) for 3 to 4½ minutes, or until the coating can be stirred smooth.

2 Dip strawberries in chocolate, one at a time; place on a baking sheet lined with wax paper. (If chocolate begins to set up during dipping, microwave at 50% (Medium) in 1-minute intervals until chocolate returns to desired consistency.) Refrigerate coated strawberries.

Total Cooking Time: 3 to 4½ minutes

How to Melt Chocolate

Place desired amount of chocolate in small bowl. Microwave at 50% (Medium) as directed in chart (below), or until chocolate is glossy and can be stirred smooth, stirring after first 2 minutes, then after each minute.

Microwave at 50% (medium)		Time:
Chocolate Chips	1 cup	2½-3½ min.
Baking Chocolate	1 square	2½-3 min.
	2 squares	2½-3¾ min.
	4 squares	3½-4½ min.

Quick Chocolate Fondue

1 can (16½ oz.) prepared chocolate frosting
1 to 2 tablespoons defrosted orange juice concentrate
Fondue dippers (cake pieces or fruit pieces)

About 2 cups

1 Place frosting in a 1-quart bowl. Microwave at High for 1 to 2 minutes, or until frosting melts, stirring once during cooking time.

2 Stir until frosting is smooth. Blend in orange juice concentrate. Serve with fondue dippers.

Total Cooking Time: 1 to 2 minutes

Elegant Touch:
Try substituting ¼ cup Amaretto or orange liqueur for the orange juice concentrate.

Nifty Tricks with Chocolate

Mint Pattie Icing:
Top each of 6 chocolate wafers or sugar cookies with 1 cream-filled chocolate mint pattie. Arrange in a circle on a plate. Microwave at 50% (Medium) for 1 to 2 minutes, or until the chocolate is glossy, rotating dish 2 or 3 times during cooking. Spread the softened patties with a spatula. Let patties cool until hardened.

Chocolate Syrup:
In a 4-cup measure, combine ⅓ cup instant chocolate-flavored drink mix, ¼ cup dark or light corn syrup, and 2 tablespoons water. Microwave at High for 45 seconds to 2 minutes, or until mixture boils. Microwave for 1 minute longer, watching closely to avoid boil-over. Chill until mixture thickens.

Chocolate Curls:
Place half of a 4-oz. block of sweet baking chocolate on a plate. Microwave at 30% (Medium Low) for 30 seconds to 1¼ minutes, or until chocolate is just barely warm to the touch, rotating dish and turning chocolate over once during the cooking time. To form curls, hold chocolate upright on its edge. With a vegetable peeler, pull across the edge of the chocolate in a continuous, even motion.

Easy Caramel Sauce

28 caramel candies (½ lb.)
¼ cup half-and-half or milk

About 1 cup

Combine the ingredients in a small bowl. Microwave at High for 2 to 4 minutes, or until the caramel is melted, stirring after every minute of cooking time.

Total Cooking Time: 2 to 4 minutes

Short-cut Hot Fudge Sauce

1 cup chocolate chips (semi-sweet or milk chocolate)
½ cup marshmallow cream
¼ cup milk

About 1 cup

Combine all ingredients in a 2-cup measure. Microwave at 50% (Medium) for 2 to 3 minutes, or until the mixture is smooth, stirring once during cooking time. (For thinner sauce, add more milk in small quantities.) Serve sauce warm or cold.

Total Cooking Time: 2 to 3 minutes

◄ Short-cut Hot Fudge Peanut Sauce

1 cup chocolate chips (semi-sweet or milk chocolate)
¼ cup peanut butter
¼ cup milk

About 1 cup

Combine all ingredients in a 2-cup measure. Microwave at 50% (Medium) for 2 to 3 minutes, or until the mixture is smooth, stirring once during cooking time. (For a thinner sauce, add more milk in small quantities.) Serve sauce warm or cold.

Total Cooking Time: 2 to 3 minutes

Cherry Dessert Sauce ▲

1 can (21 oz.) cherry pie filling
¼ cup kirsch (or Amaretto)

About 3 cups

Combine the ingredients in a 1-quart casserole or 4-cup measure. Microwave at High for 2 to 4 minutes, or until mixture is heated, stirring after half the cooking time. Serve with ice cream.

Total Cooking Time: 2 to 4 minutes

Variations:

Apple Dessert Sauce:
Follow recipe for Cherry Dessert Sauce, except: substitute 1 can (21 oz.) apple pie filling, ½ teaspoon ground cinnamon and ¼ cup apple juice, for cherry pie filling and kirsch. Microwave as directed.

Blueberry Dessert Sauce:
Follow recipe for Cherry Dessert Sauce, except: substitute 1 can (21 oz.) blueberry pie filling and ¼ cup prepared lemonade, for cherry pie filling and kirsch. Microwave as directed.

INDEX

CY DeCOSSE INCORPORATED
Chairman: Cy DeCosse
President: James B. Maus
Executive Vice President: William B. Jones

Design, Production & Photography:
  Cy DeCosse Incorporated
Art Directors: Bill Nelson, Bill Jones
Project Managers: Lynette Reber, Sue Kersten
Home Economists: Peggy Lamb, Jull Crum,
  Kathy Weber
Production Manager: Jim Bindas
Assistant Production Manager: Julie Churchill
Copy Editor: Bryan Trandem
Typesetting: Jennie Smith, Linda Schloegel
Production Staff: Yelena Konrardy, Lisa
  Rosenthal, David Schelitzche, Cathleen
  Shannon, Nik Wogstad, Michelle Joy
Photographers: Tony Kubat, John
  Lauenstein, Mette Nielsen
Food Stylists: Teresa Rys, Susan Sinon,
  Suzanne Finley, Robin Krause,
  Susan Zechmann
Production Consultant: Christine Watkins
Special Microwave Consultant:
  Barbara Methven
Color Separations: La Cromolito
Printing: R. R. Donnelley & Sons (0790)